Sir Henry Fowler

John Kyte

© 2014 John Kyte
First published in 2014 by the Vale of Evesham Historical Society

The Almonry Heritage Centre
Abbey Gate
Evesham
Worcestershire
WR11 4BG

John Kyte has asserted his moral right to be identified as the author of this work

All rights reserved. Apart from any fair dealing for the purpose of private study, research, criticism or review, as permitted under the Copyright, Designs and Patents Act 1988, no part of this publication may be reproduced, stored in any retrieval system or transmitted in any form or by any means, electronic, electrical, chemical, mechanical, optical, photocopying, recording or otherwise, without the prior written permission of the copyright owner. Enquiries should be addressed to the publishers.

Designed and typeset in Garamond by David Snowden

Front cover: The "Kings Own" No.6161, Royal Scot Locomotive (by kind permission of The Kings Own Royal Regiment Museum) and Sir Henry's Coat of Arms.

Plate 1: 4-6-0 "Royal Scot" No 6100 Euston to Northampton express at Berkhampsted 3rd July 1939
Plate 2: Royal Scot Class 4-6-0 "Kings Own" No.6161

ISBN 978-1-291-91427-6

Sir Henry Fowler   John Kyte

PLATE 1

PLATE 2

Foreword

Sir Henry Fowler was a remarkable man; a true polymath in every sense of the word. As far as his mechanical engineering expertise is concerned, he followed in the very distinguished footsteps of earlier engineers such James Watt, Isambard Kingdom Brunel and the father and son George and Robert Stephenson, although the name of Henry Fowler is not nearly as well known. He lived at a time of great expansion of the railway system in this country and was able to make one of the most notable contributions to its development, not only by the design of steam locomotives but also by his undoubted ability to manage a large organisation. He was the inspiration behind many of the most significant and innovative designs of steam locomotive at the time and led teams of designers and draughtsmen with a great deal of skill and competence.

Although mechanical engineering was the main thrust of Sir Henry's work, particularly in respect of the design and development of locomotive engines and the management of railway systems, he was also very interested in metallurgy especially applications of new materials. It is very clear from his presidential address to the Institution of Mechanical Engineers in 1927 that he was very aware that progress in engineering design depended on the introduction of new materials, especially metals, able to withstand higher stresses, higher temperatures as well as improved resistance to fatigue and creep. On reading his address, present-day engineers may well find the choice of materials which was available at the time to be very restrictive, but Sir Henry was one of the leaders in the promotion of new materials and he displayed expert knowledge of the subject.

As well as his main work in engineering and management, Sir Henry also found time for a host of other activities. He was clearly a very energetic person who seemed to be totally committed to every endeavour he undertook, be in Church, taking Bible classes, in sport, education, as a Justice of the Peace and the wellbeing of his employees and acquaintances. He was also a devoted family man who spent as much time as he could with his wife and children.

Sir Henry Fowler was not only one of the finest engineers of his generation, his achievements, although largely forgotten, were outstanding and deserve to be more widely known. This publication is therefore very opportune and describes his life, his work, his triumphs and his struggles. His contribution to progress in engineering and management both in peacetime and wartime cannot be overestimated. He is indeed someone of whom the people of Evesham can be justifiably proud.

Professor Robert Davies
March 2014

Contents

Foreword iv

Sir Henry Fowler. KBE, CBE, LLD, DSc. Introduction 1

Chapter 1: An Evesham Family..3

Chapter 2: The Track to the Future...10

Chapter 3: Chief Mechanical Engineer of the Midland Railway 1910 to 1914..18

Chapter 4: The work as Chief Mechanical Engineer Midland Railway..26

Chapter 5: The Challenge of War...32

Chapter 6: Back to Derby..41

Chapter 7: New Directions..47

Chapter 8: The Demise of the Small Engine Policy..........................63

Chapter 9: Leaving the Chief Mechanical Engineer's Chair............73

Chapter 10: Journey's End..77

Chapter 11: Vale Connections..83

Appendix 1: Extracts from *Times* obituary..88

Appendix 2: Presidential chairs & positions held.............................89

Appendix 3: Presidential Address to the Institution of Mechanical Engineers 1927..90

Acknowledgements 116

Index..118

List of photographs

Photo 1: The Fowler family (courtesy of Spondon Historical Society)........6

Photo 2: Evesham LMS Station c.1906 15

Photo 3: Evesham Hockey Club at Colwyn Bay 1906 (VEHS)..................16

Photo 4: The 'Homestead' (Spondon Historical Society)............................20

Photo 5: Henry with Spondon Cricket Club, League Champions 1914 (Spondon Historical Society)..21

Photo 6: Henry Fowler (courtesy of the Institution of Mechanical Engineers)..24

Photo 7: 0-6-0 Class 4F at Derby on 22nd May 1948 (H.C. Casserley)........28

Photo 8: Restored Fowler 0-6-0 Class 4F No.44422 at Wansford (Richard Kyte)..29

Photo 9: 2-8-0 Class 7F with 0-6-0T Class 3F (David Cross)......................30

Photo 10: Fowler No's 47638, 7308 and 3433 at Bromsgrove 21st May 1948 (H Casserley)..31

Photo 11: Henry Fowler on the left in the Veteran's 50-yard sprint 35

Photo 12: Descending the Lickey incline 1952 (H. Casserley)....................42

Photo 13: The Women's Institute Hall at Spondon (Spondon Historical Society)..44

Photo 14: Spondon Hall circa 1870 (Spondon Historical Society) 45

Photo 15: The hall just before demolition in a neglected state (Spondon Historical Society)...45

Photo 16: A restored 0-6-0T 'Jinty' Locomotive 47493 on 26th April 2010 (Richard J. Kyte) 49

Photo 17: 4-4-0 Class 4 Express Passenger Engine No.1000 (Richard J. Kyte) 50

Photo 18: 4-6-0 Royal Scot Class No.6155 'The Lancer' (H.C. Casserley) 59

Photo 19: 2-6-0:0-2-6 Beyer-Garratt on a Toton to Brent coal train..........61

Photo 20: Hughes/Fowler 2-6-0 class 6P5F at Evesham 1956 (H. Casserley) 62

Photo 21: Sir Henry (left) at Spondon Fete on 28th June 1934 (Spondon Historical Society) 67

Photo 22: 0-8-0 Class 7F Mineral Engine (H.C. Casserley) 69

Photo 23: 4-6-0 Patriot Class No. 45532 'Illustrious' Northchurch (Aug. 1947) 70

Photo 24: The original signed photograph of the 'Royal Scot' presented to Prince Henry's Grammar School by Sir Henry, in 1928. 71

Photo 25: Sir Henry and Lady Fowler with Eric at his Graduation from Clare College Cambridge (Spondon Historical Society) 76

Photo 26: Sir Henry (centre) at the Bible Class Reunion 1935 (Spondon Historical Society) 78

Photo 27: Sir Henry (centre back row) at OAP Tea Party 1934 79

Photo 28: Fowler 2-6-4T Evesham to Birmingham at Broom Junction (2nd May 1947) 83

Photo 29: Hughes/Fowler 2-6-0 Class 6P5F New Street to Ashchurch (26th Sept 1959) 84

Photo 30: Fowler 2-6-4T, 9.40 a.m. Ashchurch to New Street, at Beckford (24th April 1958) 84

Photo 31: Fowler 0-6-0 Class 4F No.44422 at Wansford, Nene Valley Railway (Richard J. Kyte) 85

Photo 32: Fowler 0-6-0 Class 4F passing Bengeworth Station (which was in Hampton) (Middleton Press) 86

Photo 33: Port Street in flood c 1890. Fowlers Shop Nos. 8 & 9 (white shop front), is on right at the edge of flood line. This was Sir Henry's birthplace. Deacle's School railings can be seen just below the shop.... 116

Photo 34: Fowler's Shop in High Street c 1930 117

Sir Henry Fowler   John Kyte

Sir Henry Fowler. KBE, CBE, LLD, DSc.
Introduction

Over the years there have been a number of Vale of Evesham Historical Society publications giving accounts of people who through history, have been associated with Evesham: Simon de Montfort and Abbot Clement Lichfield being perhaps the foremost. However there is one person who was born in Evesham and very little mention of his name or achievements has been published as a local history record.

That person is Henry Fowler who was knighted in 1918 for his services to the war effort in World War One.

During the design of the Vale of Evesham Historical Society's exhibition at the Almonry Museum illustrating the 'Influence of the Industrial Revolution on the Vale', a great deal of information was collected on the life of Sir Henry Fowler, his local family, his early education at Prince Henry's Grammar School, and his contribution to the technology, engineering and education of the late 19th and early 20th century. In studying contemporary accounts, a picture is formed of a modest man who throughout his life lived up to his religious beliefs, who commanded respect both nationally and internationally in the engineering world, enjoyed sporting activities and who demonstrated his support for the communities in which he lived.

It was therefore decided to produce a local history publication about Sir Henry Fowler and his achievements in the hope that it will help to acknowledge a local man and provide a record for future generations and students. This account is an attempt to relate situations, people, establishments and events which had relevant influences on his career and life from a local history point of view. It illustrates the many successes in his career ranging from design, organisation and management in the railway industry, his massive contribution to the war effort at the Royal Aircraft Factory, the many government and academic committees on which he served and the presentation of research and development papers to engineering institutions. It also tells of his disappointments and frustrations particularly with the 'small engine policy' preferred by successive Boards of Management, of first the Midland Railway and later the London Midland and Scottish Railway.

To detail all the engineering aspects of his distinguished career would produce a volume which may overwhelm a local history record. Much of the technical information has therefore been omitted, although some salient data are included. However, certain characteristics were a feature of his entire life. These were his Christian beliefs, his beneficial actions and the importance attached to the welfare of his family, his work colleagues and the communities in which he lived.

Chapter 1: An Evesham Family

In studying the contribution to history that a person has made and to build an accurate profile of that person, it can be helpful to investigate their family background. History has shown how some of the greatest engineers and scientists came from humble family beginnings. For example: Isaac Newton whose father was a farmer, and Michael Faraday who was apprenticed to a bookbinder. The fact that Henry Fowler was born and bred in Evesham, a place not generally associated with engineering, gives an added interest to an investigation of his background.

As well as family, religion also had an influence; in this instance the Quaker movement. For example, Abraham Darby the inventor of iron smelting, Robert Stephenson railway engineer, Edward Pearse one of the founders of the Stockton and Darlington Railway, John Dalton scientist and Joseph Lister, discoverer of antiseptics were all Quakers.

No less prominent was the name of Fowler. The captain of the *Mayflower* (the Pilgrim Fathers' ship) was James Fowler. John Fowler, no direct relation, invented the double steam engine ploughing system which transformed the agricultural industry. The system was demonstrated at Worcester in 1863. He also designed a steam locomotive. A further example is the civil engineer, Sir John Fowler, 1812 to 1897, again no relation, who worked on the Great Western Railway Oxford to Worcester line and who took over responsibility following the death of Brunel.

The family history and the association with the Quakers may suggest a natural inclination to technology and design of artefacts. There have been over nine generations of Fowlers and the name Henry has followed through generation after generation. Many of these families became Quakers, although from Bengeworth parish records it would appear that the local families did not convert to the Quaker movement until the late 17th century.

It is interesting to note that Quakers were not allowed to attend universities and therefore many of them went into banking, commerce and industry, although some were involved in the beginnings of the Industrial Revolution. Quaker beliefs prevented them from engaging in any industry which could be associated with war. This particular factor could well have prevented Henry Fowler from undertaking certain work during his career as we will see later.

The name of Fowler appeared in Bengeworth parish records in 1632 although the spelling of the name was 'Fowller'; over the next 50 years another variant was written as Fouler. Other historical records show that there were Fowlers who set up business in Evesham as silk workers. Also Henry, Great Grandfather (GGF) became a Quaker and his children were brought up in that faith. Fowlers also lived in Pershore and Upton on Severn and it was the latter place in which Henry Fowler, Grandfather (GF) was born in 1840. His birthplace is given as Pershore in the census of 1851, but is given as Upton on Severn in the census of 1871. He took over his father's business circa 1830 and branched out into upholstery and furnishings; indicating that the family were talented in producing artefacts and were resourceful businessmen.

The family returned to the Church of England between 1820 and 1840. This is confirmed by Henry (GF) marrying Elizabeth Hawkes at St Peter's, Bengeworth on the 25th August 1836. Elizabeth was the daughter of Thomas Hawkes and Elizabeth, née Ford, of Bretforton. She was christened at Bretforton on 30th June 1811.

The 1851 census shows Henry and Elizabeth living at 29 Port Street, where the present general store now stands. By this time they had a large family, Elizabeth born 1837, Sarah Hawkes born 1838, George born 1840, died 1840, Winifred born 1841, Henry (F) born 1843, Jane 1845, Susan born 1847 and Ann born 1849. All the children were recorded as scholars.

Henry, father (F), spent much of his early years with relatives at Pershore and Upton, but returned to his father's business and was shown as an assistant upholsterer and cabinet maker in the census of 1861.

In 1869 he married a Welsh girl, Mary Hughes and about this time he took over the family business and opened a shop at number 8 Port Street, Bengeworth (see *Photo 33*). This building was pulled down some years ago and the site is now occupied by a hairdresser business.

Henry and Mary settled down and had a family of their own of which Henry was their first child born on 29th July 1870. He was to become the renowned engineer and is the subject of this account.

The census of 1871 reads:

Henry Fowler	*Head*	*27*	*Upholsterer.*
Mary	*Wife*	*25*	
Henry	*Son*	*8 months.*	

Henry was joined by three sisters and three brothers: Arthur born 1872, Jennie born 1874, Bessie born 1877, Hugh born 1880, Mollie born 1888 and Charles born, 1883.

The census of 1891 reads:

Henry Fowler	*Head*	*47*	*Upholsterer & Cabinet Maker.*
Mary	*Wife*	*45*	
Henry	*Son*	*20*	*Engineer Apprentice.*
Arthur	*Son*	*19*	*Artist.*
Jessica	*Dau*	*17*	
Bessie	*Dau*	*14*	*Scholar*
Hugh	*Son*	*11*	*Scholar*
Charles	*Son*	*8*	*Scholar*
Mary	*Dau*	*3*	

Photo 1: The Fowler family (courtesy of Spondon Historical Society)

Jessica	*Arthur*	*Henry*	*Bessie*
	Father	*Mother*	
Hugh	*Mary*		*Charles*

The photograph, circa 1890, shows the family sitting in the garden of their home in Port Street.

As Henry senior, had been close to the family's association with the Quakers, the discipline and morals were always observed by the family. From Henry's life we shall see how those principles applied to the family's Christian beliefs.

He did not consume alcohol and remained a teetotaller all his life. His father ensured that he had a good education and also encouraged him and his brothers in sport and healthy pursuits. They would regularly go for morning swims in the River Avon, which flowed only a short distance away from the family home near the Workman Bridge.

From the family portrait it can be seen that Henry, by now twenty years old, had a fine physique which enabled him to play an active role in many sporting activities throughout his life. These included cricket, swimming and hockey; in many of these he played at representative as well as club levels. He continued to take part in sports until the last few years of his life.

Henry's early education was at Miss Hill's, a private school in High Street in Evesham, later occupied by Mr. E.G. Righton. The subject of school uniform cropped up in Henry's school days when he gained entrance to the grammar school in 1879. Writing in the first edition of the *Henrician* in 1924, he recalls wearing his grammar school uniform on the first day in September 1879.

The earlier reference to situations regarding Quakers and war, which had an influence on Henry's career, is also relevant when he started at Prince Henry's Grammar School, Evesham. By this time Henry would have had experience of the skills used by his father in the trade of cabinet making. These included the use of design drawings and the tools and the skills of using one's hands to produce fine artefacts. It is interesting that his brother Arthur attended the Birmingham Art School and who may have become an accomplished artist had he not died as a young man. Charles his younger brother also inherited the skills of design. He became a cabinet maker and later ran the Fowler's Furniture Shop in High Street, Evesham until he retired. This shop later became the Argos retail store.

The Grammar School, with foundations looking back to the school founded by the monks of Evesham Abbey in 1377, had, after the Napoleonic wars, ceased to exist because there were no pupils. After a number of failed attempts to open the school in the 18th-century, it was finally re-established by the Rev. F.W. Holland, Vicar of Evesham, in 1879. One of the requirements of Grammar School admission was that pupils were capable of reaching a certain standard of academic achievement and that their fathers were in business in Evesham. In September of that year, Henry started his first term and studied under the tutelage of the Rev. Holland. At this time there were about thirty pupils. In 1881 the Rev. Holland appointed a new resident Headmaster, the Rev. Sealey Poole, M.A. who was a young man thirty years old and the son of a surgeon. He taught mathematics and Latin, had a great knowledge of science and from accounts possessed enthusiasm and drive. This is illustrated in an account of the 1887 Queen's Jubilee celebrations at Badsey:

> *"Lastly there was a display of fireworks from the church tower and of this the Rev. Sealey Poole (of Evesham), who manufactured his own materials, had the control..."*

Here was the very man to recognise Henry's ability and encourage him to follow a path, which as we are to see, resulted in first class results. His academic abilities in mathematics and sciences were quickly identified and because Mr Poole was an excellent mentor in those particular subjects, this was a massive advantage. From accounts of activities at the grammar school during the time in which Henry was a pupil from 1879 to 1885, there is no doubt that Mr Poole must have influenced Henry's high moral standards and his welfare concerns about other people which were maintained throughout his life.

To quote from the *Reminiscences of an Old Boy*, October 1883 to July 1886, by W.B. Sharp (*'Henrician'*, 1924):

> *"The Headmaster, the Rev. Sealy (sic) Poole, was loved and respected by all his boys. His many acts of kindness and encouragement are still fresh in my memory". "The number of boys then attending the school was 32, of whom the 3 head boys were Pittway Primus, Sturch, and Fowler Primus now Sir Henry Fowler."*

During his time at the Grammar School, Henry would have passed the two railway stations on his way to the school situated at Lanesfield on Greenhill. He would have observed the steam locomotives on a daily basis which may well have influenced his decision about a future career. By the age of fifteen, he was encouraged by his teachers to begin higher studies at the Mason Science College in Birmingham; this academic establishment later became the University of Birmingham. Here, he studied mathematics, science, metallurgy and engineering drawing. He took a great interest in metallurgy, which was due no doubt to the enthusiasm of the lecturer Mr Turner, who later became Professor Turner. It can be clearly seen that these subjects were the key to Henry's future career and an ultimate distinguished place in the engineering world.

In 1887 he received an Engineering Diploma with which he began his career in the rapidly growing Industrial Revolution. There could not have been a more opportune time.

Chapter 2: The Track to the Future

The award of the Engineering Diploma was just the beginning on the path to a future engineering career, for although the theoretical knowledge had been gained, practical skills and experience were now required. As a result of the achievements of British engineers in the mid-18th century and onwards, for example, Brunel, Newcomb, Trevithick, George and Robert Stephenson, the Industrial Revolution brought about a massive requirement for engineers.

The railway system, which was rapidly spreading nationwide, was becoming one of the biggest industries. This sector of engineering provided a first class opportunity for training and experience. The companies recruited from colleges and institutions which in many cases they also funded.

Henry Fowler, who had demonstrated his excellence in the sciences and particular interest in metallurgy, became an apprentice engineer with the Lancashire and Yorkshire Railway in 1887. This company was in the process of building new workshops, technical and administration offices at Horwich in Cheshire. In addition the Railway Mechanics Institute was to provide training in railway engineering which would be centred in a building at Chorley on a site next to the Horwich plant. With all the latest technology and support services grouped together and with the training of young engineers being available in close proximity, there was not a better situation in which to achieve the highest standards of engineering expertise.

At Horwich, as an engineering apprentice, Henry was supervised by the Chief Mechanical Engineer, John Aspinall, who took a keen interest in the apprentice engineers and encouraged them to take advantage of the excellent training and education in order to reach their full potential. Henry obtained a Whitworth Exhibition in 1891, being the first student at the establishment to receive one. He also proved how he could undertake the hard manual tasks in the workshops and through this practical work he gained a vast knowledge of the structure and workings of steam locomotives. Aspinall recognised Henry's academic and practical skills and took him under his direct supervision as an engineering pupil alongside George Hughes and Richard Maunsell, who were also destined for great achievements in the railway locomotive industry.

Aspinall had noted Henry's great interest in metallurgy and in his final year placed him under the direction George Hughes in the Test Room. This enabled him to develop his research skills which paid dividends later when Hughes became Chief Mechanical Engineer (CME) of the London Midland and Scottish Railway (LMSR) and Henry became his deputy.

There soon followed other promotions, firstly to Inspector of Materials in 1894, following Hughes move to design. Having shown an interest in gas as a form of lighting in carriages, stations, goods yards and workshops, Henry was made Gas Manager in addition to his Test Room work.

Henry's social life also blossomed in these years. In 1892 he was invited by Philip Smith, who was Chief Clerk of the Lancashire and Yorkshire Railway, to his daughter Emma's 21st birthday party in Beaufort House, Victoria Road, just a short distance from where he lived at that time. Emma and Henry began a relationship which resulted in their marriage at Trinity Church, Horwich, on the 26th June 1895. They then settled down to live in the town which had then become the home of many employees of the railway company. In 1897 Henry and Emma became parents with the birth of their son also christened Henry.

It is interesting to note that in the 1891 census for Horwich, the employment details included Mechanical Engineers and Apprentices, Locomotive Superintendents, Civil Engineers, Apprentice Millwrights and Steam Engineers as well as Railway Accountants. This truly reflects the community in which Henry Fowler now resided.

His abilities and knowledge of engineering were becoming apparent to many of his associates and in particular to John Aspinall, who proposed him for election to the Institution of Mechanical Engineers to which he was elected an Associate Member (A.M.I. Mech.E) in 1896.

At this time the automobile was beginning to appear on the roads of Britain. The vehicles needed lights for driving at night (prior to the use of dynamos and batteries) and a reliable system was required. Acetylene gas which was used to provide lighting on the railways seemed to be the answer. Henry in his position of Gas Manager was well equipped to contribute to this field of engineering and presented a paper entitled *'Acetylene Gas for Lighting'* to the Institution of Civil Engineers in 1897. His interest also extended to the use of motor transport by the railway companies. He took the opportunity to become a Member of the Institution of Automobile Engineers and maintained his interest in this branch of engineering for the rest of his life.

In 1898 Aspinall decided to carry out research into the aerodynamics of locomotives and gave Henry the task of setting up the experiments that would be needed to study this subject. As this was very new research, it appealed to Henry's enquiring mind. He gained a great deal of knowledge in this exciting field of aerodynamics and using the results of Henry's work, Aspinall wrote a paper, which he presented to the Institution of Civil Engineers in 1901. This resulted in Aspinall receiving the Watt Medal in 1902. Henry Fowler's contribution was acknowledged which enhanced his reputation as a first class engineer who was capable of original thought and analysis.

In 1900 Samuel Johnson, Locomotive Superintendent of the Midland Railway, began to look for a person to take charge of the research department which included gas projects. Fowler applied for this position with the backing of Aspinall and was successfully appointed to the position of Gas Manager. In addition he assumed responsibility for research at Derby, which indicated how his previous work at Horwich was recognised. His engineering knowledge and works experience, together with his proven research abilities, had at the age of 30, provided him with exciting opportunities for the future.

In the same year Henry, Emma and their family moved to Rose Hill Street, Derby, which was only a short distance from the Derby works and design offices were he would work.

The census of 1901 reads:

Henry Fowler	*Head*	*30 years*	*Gas Engineer.*
Emma	*Wife*	*29 years*	
Henry	*Son*	*3 years*	
Amy Price		*16 years*	*General Servant/Domestic.*

So on the 16th June 1900 he took up his new post as Gas Engineer and Chief of the Testing Department at Derby. However, following Henry's successful progression, there followed a tragic event in the Fowler family. On the 16th March 1903, Emma gave birth to a second son who was christened Geoffrey Philip, who only survived seven months, dying on the 20th October of that year. This was a devastating blow to Henry and Emma but their deep Christian faith carried them through this grievous time.

This faith was demonstrated by Henry who found time to attend religious meetings around the works and started to hold a religious service at breakfast breaks in the mess room at Derby. As we shall see, he practiced his faith throughout his life and many of his actions were for the benefit of others. This earned him great respect by many people who knew him, in particular friends and associates in Spondon, Derby, where he later lived. Examples of his care for others include letters he wrote to former members of his Bible classes when they were serving in World War I. One such letter forms part of the exhibition in the Almonry.

The year 1903 saw Johnson retire as Locomotive Superintendent, and Deeley took over the position. Over the next few years there was a great deal of unsettling management moves in an effort to establish power in the Midland Railway. In October 1904 Henry and Emma were blessed with a daughter, Dorothea, a sister for young Henry, now aged seven. At this time the family decided to move to a new home in Chelleston, Derby about three miles from the railway works.

In 1907 Henry was appointed Works Manager, and soon after he was sent to America to study their railway systems. While he was away, the Chief Locomotive Draughtsman, James Anderson, was appointed to take care of the Works Manager's duties. He was an enthusiastic promoter of the 'small engine policy' which was eventually to cause considerable criticism of the Midland Railway (MR) and London, Midland & Scottish Railway (LMS) companies. It also had a profound effect on Henry's career and life, as will become clear later in this account.

Henry took to his post of Works Manager with great enthusiasm and became a popular and well respected figure in the Derby workshops. He toured each day often dressed in overalls and riding a bicycle, looking at the work in progress and carrying out inspections of the work. Despite his large physique he would crawl inside boilers and under locomotive frames to see the standard of workmanship for himself. Because of his friendly manner as well as his engineering knowledge, he was respected by the workshop staff and achieved a good rapport with them.

An amusing situation which illustrates his zeal for satisfying himself of the quality of welding inside boilers and internal areas of locomotives, is that one day when his assistant entered his office he was most surprised to find him on the floor trying to squeeze his large frame through the back of his office chair. Henry explained that he had realised the hole in the chair back was the same as a fire hole of a certain locomotive and that if he could get through the chair, he could get into the firebox of the locomotive.

Photo 2: Evesham LMS Station c.1906

The type and size of the locomotives which were operating at this time was, for example, the 0-6-0 Johnson, as seen in *Photo 2* above.

An incident that illustrates his affable nature occurred when he was touring the works one day. As opposed to modern day health and safety requirements, he favoured wearing a straw boater hat. Imagine a large framed gentleman, in overalls and wearing a straw boater hat making his way through railway workshops riding a bicycle. On this occasion his cycle wheel became trapped in a rail track; resulting in a swift and probably undignified dismounting of his bicycle, losing his hat, and without delay replacing it, remounting and continuing on his way.

Henry was very fit and athletic and had taken part in many sports particularly hockey and as already mentioned he had played, together with his brother Charles, for Evesham Hockey Club. In *Photo 3* below the Evesham Hockey Club team are shown on tour in North Wales in 1906. Henry is in the centre in the white shirt and from the pads he is wearing it would appear that he was playing in the position of goalkeeper. His brother Charles is in the back row second from the left. It is obvious that Henry was a commanding figure and would have been a formidable obstacle to the opponents forwards! It is interesting to note that he still played for Evesham despite living in Derby. He continued to play, representing Derbyshire in the Midland Counties League, becoming an umpire and finally being elected to the English Selection Board for hockey, another honour which emanated from his Evesham upbringing.

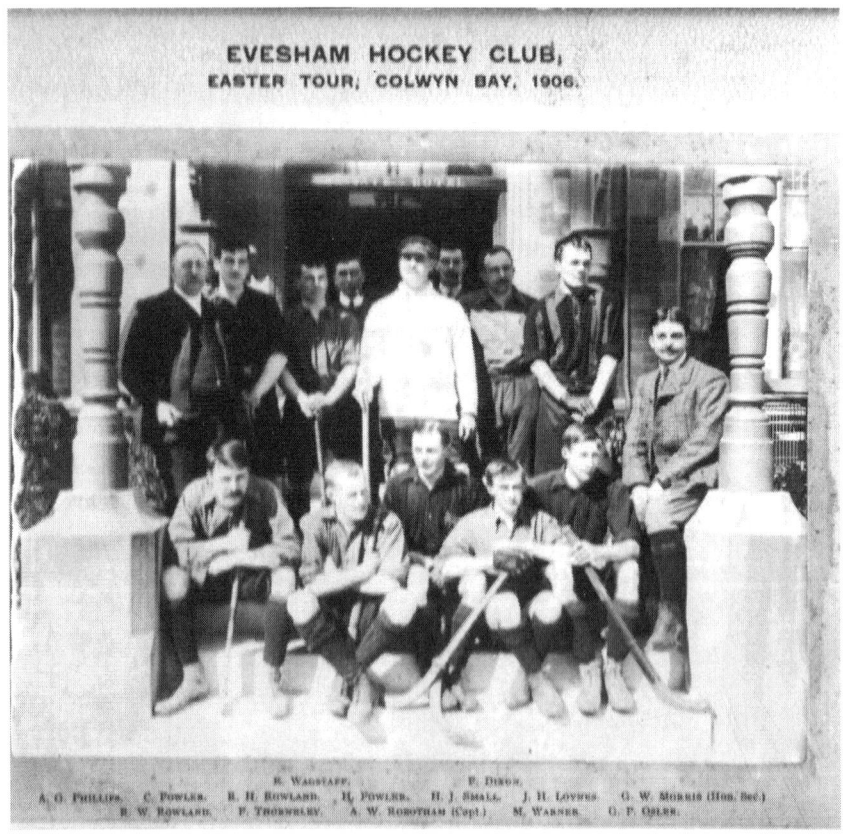

Photo 3: Evesham Hockey Club at Colwyn Bay 1906 (VEHS)

During the period 1903 to 1909 Deeley, the Locomotive Superintendent, had introduced some modified versions of earlier Johnson designs, mainly to the 0-6-0 locomotives, a redesigned compound locomotive which proved a great success, and finally a 0-6-4T tank engine for passenger services.

In 1909 further management changes were made to the top structure of the Midland Railway which resulted in Deeley resigning. It is interesting to note that at this time Deeley had just completed the design for a 4-6-0 four cylinder compound engine which would have been a complete change from the small engine policy of the MR. At the time of his resignation the design was scrapped by Anderson. This was later shown to be a poor decision and resulted in lost opportunities with regard to both engineering progress and company profitability.

Upon Deeley's departure, the Board of Directors considered for some time the best person to replace him. Henry Fowler's work and enthusiasm as Works Manager was recognised; and he was appointed Chief Mechanical Engineer of the Midland Railway on the 1st January 1910 at the age of 39.

Chapter 3: Chief Mechanical Engineer of the Midland Railway 1910 to 1914

The responsibilities of the post of Chief Mechanical Engineer (CME) illustrate the confidence in his engineering and management abilities which the Board had entrusted to Henry and which for many would have presented too daunting a task. He assumed responsibility for over 2,900 locomotives of various ages and states of maintenance, covering nearly 50 million miles a year, twenty acres of workshops and other buildings, over 6,000 employees in all engineering trades and professions and large erecting workshops capable of producing more than 70 locomotives at any one time. In addition he would have been be involved in design, planning, presenting strategy programmes for the Board of Management as well as attending conferences and representing the railway company at national and international events.

The census of 1911 schedule 74, which was filled in by Henry and carries his signature, reads:

Henry Fowler	*Head*	*40*	*Chief Mechanical Engineer Railway Company Born Evesham, Worcestershire.*
Emma Needham Fowler	*Wife*	*39*	*Born Manchester, Lancashire.*
Henry Fowler	*Son*	*13*	*Born Horwich, Lancashire.*
Dorathea Fowler	*Dau.*	*6*	*Born Derby.*

Following his promotion to CME, he received an invitation to become a member of the Association of Locomotive Engineers. Its members held similar posts in the railway industry and held regular meetings to discuss developments and other aspects of railway engineering. Henry joined the Association in the summer of 1910 and remained a member of this distinguished body for the rest of his life. He contributed a great deal to the advancement of steam, diesel and electric locomotion by writing and presenting discussion papers on research as well as serving on the committee of the Association.

On the 22nd June 1911 another son was born and christened George Eric, a brother for Henry who was now 14 and attending Oundle Public School in Northamptonshire. With this addition to the family combined with the status of his new position and the accompanying salary, Henry and Emma began to search for a suitable new home.

The village of Spondon on the outskirts of Derby proved to be the answer in as much that a large Georgian house built in the mid-18th century known as 'The Homestead' was for rent, and it proved to be the ideal property for a number of reasons. It was fairly close to the Midland Railway works which was a short drive by car or alternatively a short rail journey from Spondon station.

The village had a cricket club which had been another passion of Henry's from his early days in Evesham. Henry soon joined the cricket club and eventually became captain, later becoming President. From correspondence by members of the club who were friends of Henry, it would appear that his cricket talents did not quite match his hockey skills, but his status, age and the respect in which he was held, resulted in him being appointed captain. However for decisions in the field he relied greatly on the Vice Captain, William (Bill) Thompson, who was a leading local player of the day.

Photo 4: The 'Homestead' (Spondon Historical Society)

In *Photo 5* Bill is sitting on Henry's left. He also started Bible classes for young men in Spondon and took an interest in many activities in the village, always ready to offer his services and time in support. He was held in great esteem by the people of Spondon, whom he treated as friends; members of the Historical Society have been keen to emphasise these attributes.

At this point the Midland Railway management board decided to dispense with the post of Locomotive Superintendent and replace it with two posts: those of Chief Mechanical Engineer and Chief Motive Power Superintendent. It would appear however that the responsibilities of these posts was not clearly defined, indeed it seems likely that the MR board were not too sure themselves.

Photo 5: Henry with Spondon Cricket Club, League Champions 1914 (Spondon Historical Society)

The main centre for locomotive design and operation was Derby, where the small engine policy had been maintained causing much confusion and debate. These problems continued when the new grouping occurred in 1923 and the new London, Midland and Scottish Railway (LMS) was formed in response to current Government policy for railways.

This, then, was the environment that existed when Henry became CME. Some critics later sought to blame him for the apparent lack of locomotive power that was a feature of the MR and for allowing LMS to fall behind other railway companies who were developing more powerful engines. Henry Fowler had proved his first class engineering background, not only theoretical but with hands-on practical experience. He had been considered the brightest pupil of Aspinall's group, demonstrated his excellent research abilities and his organisational management as Works Manager. Therefore it would seem inconceivable that he did not see the need for larger locomotives.

So why was the small engine policy still being maintained at this time? There have been a number of reasons put forward by observers and historians of the railways and these could be discussed at great length, but the purpose of this publication is to give a brief account of Henry Fowler and his contribution to the engineering profession. However it would be an injustice not to provide the reader with a broad picture of the problems facing him and the challenge to his engineering talents and character.

The MR had always produced small engines on the basis of economical running suited to their Civil Engineering design works, which led to weight restrictions on the loading of track. The company had operated passenger trains of about 250 tons despite the fact that they were running heavy mineral trains which represented a large proportion of their income. This restriction of track loads imposed by the Chief Civil Engineer (similar to the restrictions experienced by Churchward; CME of the Great Western Railway) became a problem as the need for heavier goods trains as a result of the growth of the engineering industry coupled with increased passenger rail travel and new routes, put enormous strains on the company. The operating methods employed to handle the heavier loads were to double head the trains, which would appear to be an uneconomical solution.

The policy remained throughout Henry's time as CME on the Midland Railway, and as he was deemed responsible for all designs is a probable reason why he was criticised for the lack of more powerful locomotives. It would be that this conclusion was incorrect, as many distinguished engineers have pointed to a number of instances when Henry Fowler and his predecessors, Deeley and Hughes, had produced designs for more powerful locomotives, but had seen them rejected due to the policy of the management boards. For example Deeley had proposed a 4-6-0 four cylinder compound locomotive in 1909, mentioned on page 17. Henry had considered the problem of the 1-in-37 Lickey incline near Bromsgrove and proposed the design of a powerful 0-10-0 locomotive (1914/20) which would be capable of assisting the heavy goods and passenger trains up the steep hill. At times as many as 4 separate small locomotives were needed to accomplish this task! He also produced a design to further develop Deeley's 4-6-0 Compound (1924), together with a design for a 0-8-0 (1920) heavy goods locomotive. From this list it appears that he most certainly considered larger locomotive power to be the future of the railways. Some of these designs are illustrated as line drawings and are shown in following chapters. Andrew Roden, the Contributing Editor of *International Railway Journal* sums up the situation in his excellent book *The Duchesses:*

> *"The Chief Mechanical Engineers were all handicapped by this 'small engine' policy and when new locomotives were needed, the powers that be decreed that batches of Midland designed locomotives were what was really best. Every time the Chief Mechanical Engineer, Henry Fowler, prepared designs for new locomotives, the dead hand of the Midland Railway policy slapped him firmly down, led by James Anderson, the Chief Motive Power Superintendent."*

As other commentators have observed it would appear that both the Midland and later the LMS, by dismissing the designs, lost a valuable asset in locomotive development that could have paid massive dividends in future years. Indeed it was not until after Henry had left the post of CME of the LMSR that they changed their policy and accepted the need for larger locomotives post 1930.

In 1912 Henry was elected to the Presidency of the Institution of Locomotive Engineers and his Presidential Address given in 1913, 'The Maintenance and Repair of Locomotives,' displayed his already definitive knowledge of the subject. In the same year he was elected to the Presidency of the University of Birmingham Engineering Society, which had evolved from the Mason Science College at which Henry had studied after leaving Evesham Grammar School. The University quite rightly wished to honour their former student who had by now achieved a distinguished engineering position.

Photo 6: Henry Fowler (courtesy of the Institution of Mechanical Engineers)

Although he had a heavy workload, in November 1912 he joined the Association of Railway Engineers (ARLE) committee on the standards for screw threads, an important aspect of engineering. Demonstrating his forward thinking, he was behind the construction of an electric battery shunting engine built at Derby in 1913 which survived into British Rail (BR) days.

In the same year he was elected Secretary of the ARLE. In 1914 he was again elected to the Presidency of the Institution of Locomotive Engineers and the University of Birmingham Engineering Society. That year also saw his son Henry jnr. leave the public school at Oundle to join the army, despite his father and mother being concerned that he was only 17. He expressed his strong convictions to serve his country and enlisted in the Royal Engineers.

When the war started many of Henry's work colleges at Derby, together with a number of young men from his Bible Class at Spondon, were soon in action in France. Henry, displaying his care for others, began to write to them keeping them in touch with everything that was going on at home. These letters must have had a great morale boosting effect on those experiencing the horrors of war at the front and in the trenches. Letters written towards the end of the war gave the latest news from home and are shown in a later chapter. These letters are by the courtesy of Dennis Cameron, whose father Ken is mentioned in one letter.

Chapter 4: The work as Chief Mechanical Engineer Midland Railway

In this chapter a brief technical summary is given of some of the locomotive designs for which Henry Fowler was responsible as Chief Mechanical Engineer. The interpretation of "designer" is always open to debate. In the case of the Chief Mechanical Engineer he would issue instructions for the design requirements to senior draughtsman who would then produce draft designs which the CME would normally accept or refer back for modifications. The CME would have the technical knowledge and experience to satisfy himself that the final design met the requirements of the client, in this case the Railway Board of Management. Other examples of this convention are the CMEs of the Great Western Railway, G.J. Churchward and C. Collett.

Much of the work load which Henry Fowler inherited on becoming CME was concerned with the maintenance of locomotives, many of which had seen decades of service. In addition, modifications and redesigns of his predecessor's engines to meet heaver demands as well as the design of some new locomotives were part of his responsibilities.

In order to illustrate the development of locomotives without becoming too technical the following data is given to enable the reader to appreciate the designs and performance during his term as CME.

> **Tractive Effort (TE):** Expressed in pounds (or kilograms) as nominal tractive effort. It is worked out from a mathematical formula. It establishes the theoretical backward push exerted on the driving wheels on the rail track, with the locomotive in full gear and with maximum

boiler pressure assuming no other loss between wheels and track. Example: 25,000lbs.

Wheel Arrangement: Notation showing the number of driving wheels in the centre, the leading wheels before and the trailing wheels after. Example: 0-6-0.

Classification of Power: From 1 to 10. P= Passenger, F= freight. Example: 4F.

The Midland Railway had a large amount of its business in freight traffic, in particular the movement of coal from Toton to Brent. To move these heavy loads they used 0-6-0 engines which were introduced in 1885 (Johnson) and 1906 (Deeley). They were not superheated, had limited power (T.E. 19890 lbs) and had to be double-headed most of the time. These were rebuilt by Henry in 1911 by improving the design of these engines with the use of more efficient Belpaire fireboxes.

In 1911, the design of these engines was modified under Henry's supervision by the use of more efficient Belpaire fireboxes and by the incorporation of new technology including superheating, which was of great personal interest, and which resulted in a very excellent locomotive which continued to be built until 1941. This locomotive was classified as 0-6-0 Class 4F and a total of 722 were produced; it was considered to be one of the most successful of his designs. This class of locomotive was seen regularly on the fruit freight trains and other goods trains at Evesham. T.E. 24555 lbs. 4F

Photo 7: 0-6-0 Class 4F at Derby on 22nd May 1948 (H.C. Casserley)

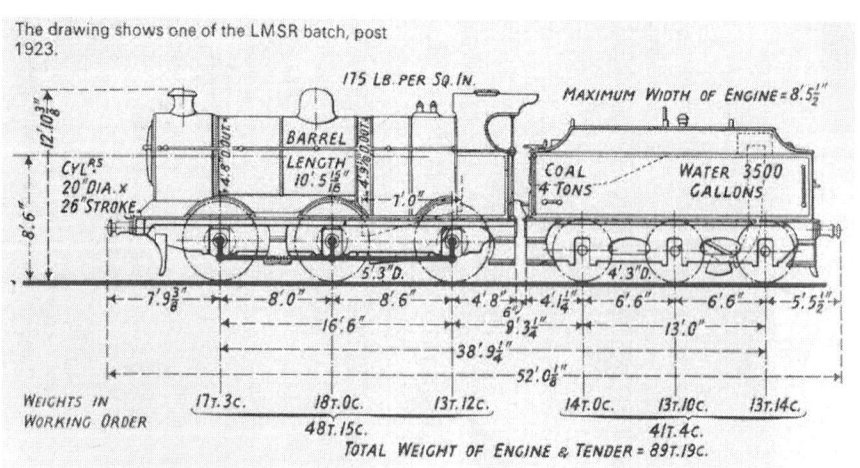

Line Drawing of 0-6-0 4F 1923 (courtesy of the Railway Gazette)

Photo 8: Restored Fowler 0-6-0 Class 4F No.44422 at Wansford (Richard Kyte)

It is interesting to note that when the LMSR company was formed in 1923 (see Chapter 7) the Board of Directors reviewed all the locomotives they inherited from the original companies to ascertain the quantity and performances of the different classes. Their need was to be able to provide the right locomotives to meet specific requirements that existed at that time. One of the priorities was for a freight locomotive capable of hauling heavy loads. After much consideration, it was agreed that the Midland 4F 0-6-0 was still the best of its class and the decision was made to continue building this locomotive. When Stanier became CME he considered that these locomotives could not be bettered and continued to construct them until 1941.

Following the leasing of the Somerset and Dorset Joint Railway (S&DJR) to the Midland Railway in 1876, it became apparent that the heavy mineral trains which had to tackle the steep inclines of the Mendip Hills placed a massive strain on the 0-6-0 locomotives which were then used. This meant using double-headed trains which was both uneconomical and heavy on maintenance. Henry

Fowler directed his senior draughtsman to draw up a 2-8-0 heavy locomotive which was the most powerful mineral engine on all the railways at that time. It was introduced in 1914 with a total of 11 being built for use on S&DJR with a T.E. 35295 lbs classification 7F (*Photo 9*).

During this time Henry gave a great deal of thought to the problems of the steep gradient at Lickey Hill, Bromsgrove, on the main line from the South to Birmingham and the Midlands. Many readers will no doubt know this stretch of the line and have probably travelled it and appreciated the massive incline and the locomotive power needed to haul a heavy passenger or goods train over its length. The method that was employed, which was uneconomical to say the least, was to use banking engines; two or three and on odd occasions four were required to overcome the incline (*Photo 10*).

Photo 9: 2-8-0 Class 7F with 0-6-0T Class 3F (David Cross)

Henry initiated a number of design studies for a suitable powerful locomotive which would cope with heavy loads of the order of 500 tons. However, the beginning of the war brought a halt to further progress until 1918, when the solution was the design and construction of the Lickey Banker.

Photo 10: Fowler No's 47638, 7308 and 3433 at Bromsgrove 21st May 1948 (H Casserley)

Chapter 5: The Challenge of War

For many years following the Boer War, Britain had assigned few resources to the military budget and consequently had few armaments and low troop levels when Germany, who had spent massive amounts on building their armed forces, began the hostilities which led to World War I. It soon became apparent that not only did Britain have insufficient stocks of weapons to defend itself; there was no effective organisation to produce the amount that was to be required. This was the problem facing the Prime Minister, Lloyd George, and he immediately formed the Ministry of Munitions whose task was to identify the expertise in all fields from industry, science and administration, to quickly and efficiently organise the production of the armaments.

Both Henry and Emma became involved in local groups and activities in support of the men from Spondon who had left to fight in the war. Emma helped the Spondon Women's Institute to prepare and send food parcels to the men on active service in France. Henry began to write letters to members of the Spondon Bible Class and colleagues to give them moral support and keep them up to date with home news and events. Despite his very intensive workload he always made time to write personal letters to all the men, such was typical of his concern for their welfare throughout the duration of the war.

It was at this point that Henry's engineering, research and organisational talents were recognised as fulfilling many of the requirements necessary in the defence of the nation from the might of the German war machine. The task was massive, so much was needed to even match the armed forces' requirement for weapons and ammunition to fight, what was at that stage, a land-based campaign in Europe. The call to Henry must have been somewhat of a surprise in as much as the task was in an area of munitions. However, it would be shown that he was more than capable of carrying out the job of Director of Munitions, responsible for the organisation and production of weapons and the associated materials. He had a first class asset in that railway workshops contained the heavy engineering plant and workforce skills that could be matched to the production of military guns, tanks and vehicles, and if properly organised and managed could meet the required levels of output. His influence and contacts in the railway engineering industry, backed by his undoubted organisational skills enabled him to develop these plants into efficient and powerful production units. Railway records from Derby state that he was seconded to the Ministry of Munitions on 13th June 1915 at a salary of £2,500.

This initiative resulted in a rapid increase in the production of armaments. Henry continued to motivate every factory together with any workshops which could be converted to the production of materials and equipment. Figures illustrate the success of the organisation Henry had produced: In early 1915 the number of shells produced was about 70,000, but in a matter of some six months this had increased to nearly 240,000. This outstanding effort was being noted at the Ministry and led to further advancement when Henry was promoted to the office of Superintendent of the Royal Aircraft Factory at Farnborough, the first civilian to hold the post. He commenced this new role on the 21st September 1916 and immediately began to build a positive understanding with the workers as he did in his days at Derby, encouraging them to work as an effective team in the production of a fighter aircraft for the newly formed Royal Flying Corps. Not only did he devote himself to the work, but he placed great emphasis on the welfare of all the people at Farnborough. This was an example of good industrial relations which had been so neglected in the old Victorian industry. He also promoted good relations with the local community by holding regular meetings with councillors and local organisations, in order to keep them in touch with what was being achieved at the factory.

At the time of Henry's arrival, urgent design work was being carried out to produce a fighter aircraft that could match the German fighters. Known as the SE5a aircraft, a design by H.P. Follard was being developed. This aircraft would be capable of dive speeds of up to 300m.p.h.which would give the SE5a a performance equal to the German planes. Henry recognised that Follard was the expert in this task and typically acknowledging this fact, gave Follard complete control over design and development while he concentrated on the reorganisation and the management of the factory to ensure that production could be maximised.

In 1916, King George V visited Farnborough on an official visit and Henry had the honour as Superintendent to show him around the aircraft factory which at that time was in the process of his planned reorganisation. Reports of the visit state that both men got on extremely well; striking up a personal friendship which was to last throughout the King's reign. On this occasion Henry wore his customary straw boater as he did in his Derby days. Shortly afterwards, Henry received the CBE for his services to the war effort.

Despite engine problems and a structural failure in the wing of the SE5a, which tragically resulted in the death of the test pilot and the resignation of Follard, the production of the first SE5a fighters began in March 1917. Henry soon had many firms, including Austin, Wolseley, Vickers and the Royal Aircraft Factory, setting up production lines. His motivation was to stem the losses to the allies' fighters by the then superior German aircraft, as well as preventing the bombing raids of ports and munitions factories.

There can be little doubt that his style of management and his respect for the workers brought about equal admiration and respect in return. He participated in some of the few social events which were organised to help maintain morale, despite the enormous demands for output of aircraft and other equipment. A report in *Flight Magazine* dated the 6th September 1917 of the RAF Sports day contains a photograph of Henry Fowler making a fine bid to secure a place in the Veterans 50-yard sprint, aged 47. He still maintained his fitness and competitive spirit from his early days in Evesham.

Photo 11: Henry Fowler on the left in the Veteran's 50-yard sprint

For his work and contribution to a successful campaign against the might of the German Forces, which turned the war in favour of Britain, Henry received a knighthood at an investiture by King George V at Buckingham Palace on 20th February 1918. He was also made an honorary Lieutenant-Colonel. He describes the investiture in one of his letters dated 25th March 1918 written at the Hotel Cecil in the Strand, London to George, the church warden of Spondon, who was still on active service.

> *"I got formally knighted on February 20th and found it very interesting; the King struck me on both shoulders. I got a silver star to wear on my left breast, as well as the Order to wear round my neck."*

The *Evesham Journal* gave the following brief report:

> *Sir Henry Fowler*
>
> *The King held an investiture of the Most Excellent Order of the British Empire on Wednesday. Among those introduced into the presence of his Majesty and invested with the Insignia of the respective*

divisions of the order into which they had been admitted, was Lieut.-Col. Henry Fowler, Knight Commander of the Order.

An article dated 31st January 1918 in *Flight Magazine*, sums up the warm affection in which Henry was held, in the account of a reception held just prior to his leaving Farnborough:

> "The extraordinary way in which Lieut.-Colonel Sir Henry Fowler, K.B.E., won his way to the hearts of the workers at the Royal Aircraft Factory was demonstrated in a most emphatic manner a few evenings ago when he was presented with a silver tea and coffee service and kettle, in token for all he had been to the workers, of all his understanding and of the human interest he had taken in every phase of their life. There was a large gathering of the workers in the new canteen , which is one of the improvements effected in the factory during the 15 or 16 months that Sir Henry Fowler had been Superintendent, the chair being taken by Mr. P.A. French, who is Chairman of the Organised Trade Committee, through whom the presentation was made. Mr French said he was quite unable to enumerate all the different acts Sir Henry Fowler had done which made for greater comfort in their work, but he instanced three which were appreciated by the workers; firstly, increased accommodation; secondly, the way he met them on questions concerning work in the factory; and thirdly, the way in which the coal shortage was met last winter. The formal presentation was made by the Rev. Basil Phillips, and Sir Henry Fowler, who was given a rousing reception, said his greatest regret, his whole regret, in parting was that he would not be able to keep in such close touch with them, his friends at Farnborough. Like everyone else he had been a worker, and he hoped to continue to be a worker to the end. He had said many times that apart from any question of whether it is right or wrong, no man worked, and I believe no girl worked as well as they would, without working as comfortably as they could be, not only during working hours, but in the hours that come afterwards. After all said and done, he thought what he had been able to do was very little indeed compared with what he should have been able to do. He

thanked them with all his heart not only for the very handsome present, but for what he valued much more, their friendship and kindness to him during the time he had been at Farnborough."

In March 1918, Sir Henry was promoted to Deputy Director-General of Aircraft Production which gave rise to more duties among which were representing the Ministry of Munitions on the Aircraft Mission to the USA and Canada, the Chairmanship of the Conference on Standardisation of Aircraft Components and membership of the Advisory Committee for Aeronautics. These positions indicate that by this time he had reached the top levels in aircraft and mechanical engineering, as well as organisational abilities of the highest order. Despite this heavy work load he still found time to take part in activities and technical discussions at the ARLE on the design and development of locomotives. Also in 1918 he was elected to the Council of the Institution of Mechanical Engineers.

All his successful work during the war years was recognised by the Government who offered him a peerage. However, Sir Henry decided not to accept this honour as it was hereditary which would mean that on his death all his estate would pass to his eldest son leaving nothing for Emma and his other children. Although he considered this offer to be the greatest honour, he declined with polite dignity.

His coat of arms which had been designed by the College of Arms London shows the SE5a aircraft on a centre blue shield above which is a knight's helmet surmounted by a bullet and a peregrine falcon, representing no doubt, the speed of the aircraft in a dive, enabling it to inflict great losses on the German aircraft.

Thus a very important part of Sir Henry's brilliant career came to a conclusion.

In all this time he and Emma had continued their support of the local men of Spondon, with Henry typing his own letters in what little spare time he had to himself. His care for the welfare of other people which he maintained throughout his life is shown clearly in two letters he wrote in March and May 1918 to George Wright the church warden who was on active service. In a letter dated 25th March 1918 (see full text on page 40) written from Hotel Cecil, Strand, London, Sir Henry shows his deep Christian faith, compassion and concern for people. In the opening paragraph he writes:

> *"I am late again in writing to you, and I am afraid my letter may be slow in getting across owing to the battle, which we are all praying earnestly may turn in our favour". "I was at Spondon on March 17th and took 'the Class' (reference to the Bible Class that he founded) and had a very enjoyable time. I was so delighted to see so many, as although I know that the first class from the school has had to come down, I hardly expected over 20 as there was."*

He goes on to relate all the news about the village people, their health, fellow soldiers at the front, those who have been injured and their progress.

Another letter this time written from his home, 'The Homestead', Spondon, dated 23rd May, tells of a new job which he is to take up but cannot reveal details. He goes on to give a report on many of the Spondon men who have been injured in action and their progress and in particular "three of our fellows" who had sustained serious wounds, including one who had been hit in both legs, another with shrapnel in hand and elbow and the third who was hit in the spine. Sir Henry had been in touch with all the wounded men expressing his great concern. He adds a handwritten postscript:

> *"Thank you for your note. It leads me to quote the account of the King on the back. Lady Fowler saw your daughter the other day said what a nice girl she was getting"*

The quote referred to in the letter shows how the King and Sir Henry had a very warm friendship and was copied to his friends in Spondon.

"Some of you have, I believe seen an account of my going to Lincoln with the King and Queen, but as some may not have done so I will tell you shortly. On the way there I met an American Captain. The following day I found out that he could be presented to the King, and a big push I got hold of him. I presented him and his sergeant to the King and Queen, and at once he whipped out an envelope and asked the Queen to sign it. This she did on the Sergeants back, and he then asked the King to do so. The King said 'What am I to sign on?', and so I said 'Have my back Sir'. He did so, but the American's pen would not work, and so I whipped mine out of my pocket and said 'try an English one Sir'. It was great and the American Captain was very set up. The papers had it all in."

```
       I am continuing this after all,for it is now settled
up that I am going to America in a few days, and so it will be
some little while before I am able to write again, although I
do not think I shall be over there very long.

       Some of you have, I believe, seen an account of my
going to Lincoln with the King and Queen, but as some may not have
done so I will tell you shortly.  On the way there I met an
American Captain.  The following day I found out that he could
be presented to the King, and after a big push I got hold of him.
I presented him and his Sergeant to the King and to the Queen,
and he at once whipped out an envelope and asked the Queen to
sign it.  This she did on the Sergeant's back, and he then asked
the King to do so.  The King said "What am I to sign on", and
so I said "Have my back, Sir".  He did so, but the American's
pen would not work, and so I whipped mine out of my pocket and
said "Try an English one, Sir".  It was great and the American
Captain was very set up.  The papers had it all in.

       I am at home on and off, but now am just back from Paris.

       I find that on Whit Tuesday they had a "Village Walk".
A lot of people set off to go round Locko Park.  Captain Drury
Lowe said they could go anywhere as long as they did not break
down the trees.  George Thompson ran his dray for some of the
little ones as far as the Park Gates.  It went off all right
until they got well into the Park, when they had a tremendous
thunderstorm.  It was unfortunate for it was a very good idea
and got the folks together.
```

Sir Henry's type written account of the loan of the pen to the King

Sir Henry had a great sense of humour which had been seen by all people he had come into contact with in work and in the wider community. These letters were just two of the many he wrote during the war and however busy he was on vitally important war work, he made time to think and support others, particularly those wounded on active service. One of these letters to George Wright, a churchwarden at Spondon is shown below.

These copies were kindly supplied by Dennis Cameron of Spondon, who sums up the value to the community:

> "The letters do I think show how interested Sir Henry was in the people he knew in his association in various village activities he attended i.e. the cricket club, the church etc."

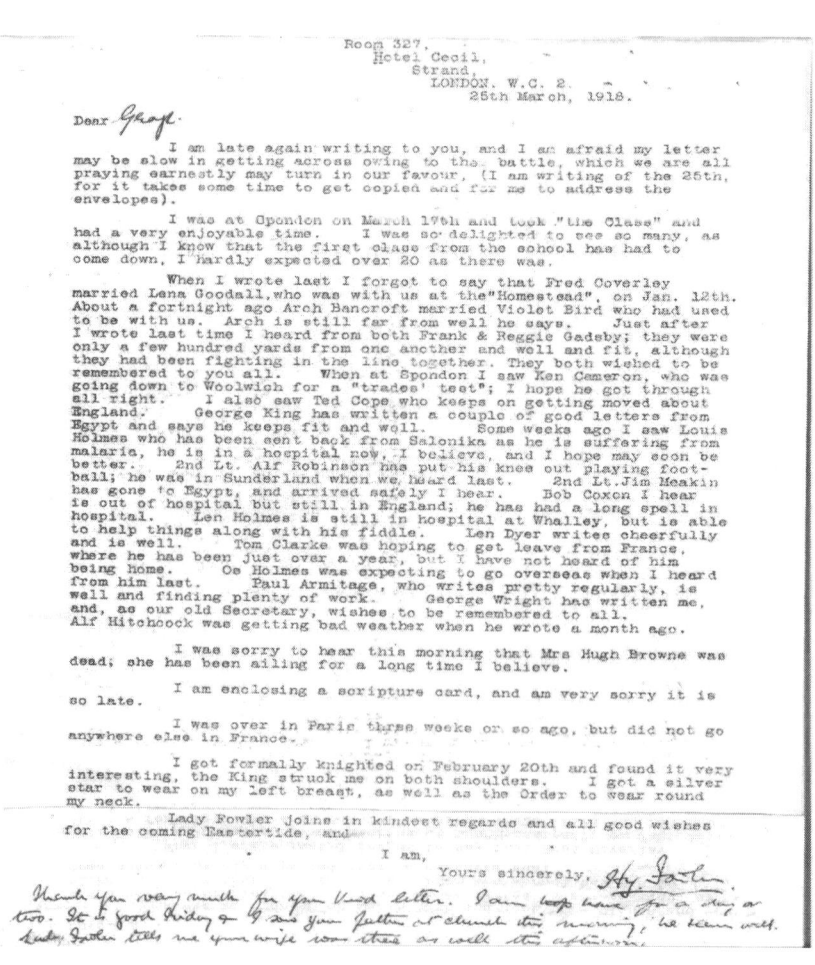

Copy of Henry's letter to George Wright, March 1918

Chapter 6: Back to Derby

It was some time, on 31st May 1919 to be precise, before Sir Henry was to return to the Midland Railway and resume the post as Chief Mechanical Engineer. Railway records state that his salary ceased to be charged to the Government at £3,500. He would probably have wondered what new challenges he would be faced with after the four years absence. He found that there had been little production of locomotives during the later war years owing, he might have reflected, to a measure of his success at Derby, in overseeing production of munitions and equipment for the war effort.

His first task was to ascertain the requirements for locomotives and resources, in order that the Midland Railway would meet the demand of both freight and passenger numbers after the war. One of the most urgent tasks was to return to the Lickey incline problem which was now acute and to which he had considered a number of options before giving the go ahead for the Derby drawing office to produce the design of a 0 10 0 tender locomotive. The construction of this locomotive began in 1914, but was disrupted by the war. By now the heavy freight trains that needed to move industrial materials required additional 'banker' engines to assist them to climb the steep 1 in 37 incline from Bromsgrove Station to Blackwell on the Bristol to Birmingham line serving the industrial Midlands. This was proving very expensive in the inefficient use of manpower, fuel and maintenance costs, a problem that Sir Henry (with his vast of knowledge and experience) would have been very aware. He immediately restarted construction of this locomotive which was completed in December, just a few months after his return to Derby. This locomotive was the most powerful in Britain and really eclipsed the 'small engine policy' of the Midland Railway.

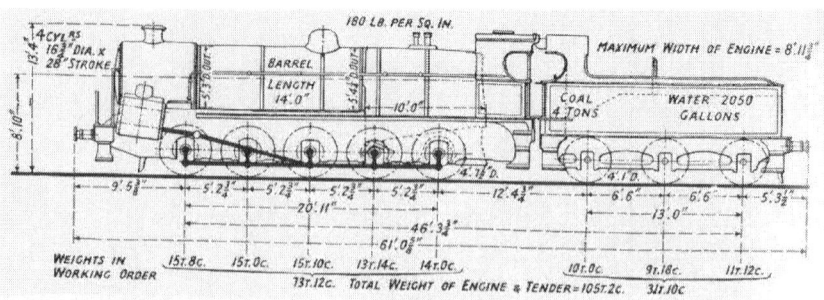

Line Drawing of 0-10-0, Lickey Banker (Courtesy *Rail Magazine*)

Photo 12: Descending the Lickey incline 1952 (H. Casserley)

The locomotive gained the nickname of 'Big Bertha' and with a weight of 105 tons, length of 61 feet and a tractive effort of 44,030 lbs it performed the task of propelling the heavy freight trains up the Lickey Incline from 1919 until it was withdrawn from service in 1956. This locomotive represented the best of British engineering.

Sir Henry demonstrated his drive and energy, a benefit of his physical and mental fitness, by not only being fully occupied at Derby but also being elected to be the President of the Institution of Automobile Engineers for the year 1920. It is interesting to note that the retiring President, Thomas Clarkson, observed:

> *"I feel particularly happy in retiring from the Presidential Chair knowing that Sir Henry Fowler has taken my place, because I am sure that the Institution could not be piloted by a better man than Sir Henry Fowler, who has by sheer merit and ability won himself a very high place in British engineering and he occupies the post, as you know, of Chief Mechanical Engineer of the Midland Railway."*

At the same time Henry was working on a paper on the subject of superheating for presentation to the Institution of Mechanical Engineers in 1922. In addition he became President of Derby Hockey Club, a school governor and continued with his Bible classes as well as occasional visits to his family in Evesham.

On his return to live at the 'Homestead' in 1919, the owners expressed the desire to sell the house so Henry and Emma decided to move to Darley Dale, but within two years he bought Spondon Hall. The family therefore returned to the village that they so loved and the activities with which they had been associated, for example the Bible class, which Henry had founded, the cricket and football clubs and Emma's work with the Women's Institute.

He also set up and coached the Bible Class football team which played in the Derby Sunday School League. His involvement with the church of St Werburgh's at Spondon led him to take up bell ringing and he eventually became Captain of the Bell Ringers. It can be seen that he retained his interest in the social activities of his community and gave his support to all other aspects of village life. A letter received from Pam Stevens, the Chairman of the Spondon Historical Society, really expresses the high regard in which he was held by the people of Spondon.

Photo 13: The Women's Institute Hall at Spondon (Spondon Historical Society)

The following extracts of Pam's letter dated 16th January 2009 illustrate the point:

> *"...he was very much esteemed in Spondon, taking an active part in all aspects of village affairs, especially the church and Cricket Club, where he was once captain. He was also a very generous benefactor. He gave the newly formed Women's Institute a piece of land from his estate in the 1920's to build their own meeting hall. He lived in Spondon from 1910 to 1919 in the Homestead, when it was for sale he wanted to buy it, but for some reason the sale fell through. He moved to Darley Dale in Derbyshire, but within two years he bought Spondon Hall, where he lived until his death. As you will see through the copies of the enclosed letters he kept in touch with the former members of the Bible class who were fighting in France during the war years. Although I was too young to know him myself, I feel very much that he was a great benefactor and was always much referred to in my childhood."*

Photo 14: Spondon Hall circa 1870 (Spondon Historical Society)

Photo 15: The hall just before demolition in a neglected state (Spondon Historical Society)

An old print of Spondon Hall circa 1870 shows what a fine estate Henry and Emma bought in 1921 befitting Sir Henry's status. The church of St Werburgh was very close to the hall. The hall was demolished in the 1960s and the grounds divided by the new A52 bypass. One of the streets built on the land is named Fowler Avenue.

In 1921 Sir Henry became the President of the Association of Railway Engineers while at the same time he served a second year as President of the Institution of Automobile Engineers. The following year he was elected a Vice President of the Institution of Mechanical Engineers. These were great honours which clearly show how some of the most prestigious engineering bodies recognised his abilities and services to engineering. The year 1923 saw him and his friend Richard Maunsell, who was CME of the South Eastern and Chatham Railway and later CME of the Southern Railway, co-operate on experiments for oil fired locomotives on which subject they presented a paper to the International Railway Congress held in Rome in 1922.

In 1921 the government passed the railway grouping legislation which was to bring together the many different railway companies into four main companies. No more new designs were pursued pending a decision on the number and types of locomotives the new grouping might require.

Henry at this time began to encourage his family to take up cycling which he had always had a passion for (remember the cycle was his form of transport around the Derby works in his early days as Works Manager). In particular his son Eric, who was now 11 years old, would accompany him on his travels. These were not only trips in this country but also trips to France, which shows that in addition to the many tasks and events in which he was involved, he still had the energy to participate in strenuous exercise.

Chapter 7: New Directions

In 1916 the Government began to consider how railways should operate after the war. Three years later a Select Committee stated that "a unification of the railways was desirable". A White Paper then proposed that the 123 railway companies should be amalgamated into seven; a clear indication of the number of different standards, designs, management organisations and inefficiency of the railways of Britain that existed at that time.

The Railway Act became law on 19th August 1921 legislating that the reorganisation was to be completed by 1st January 1923. On this date the four major companies were formed. These were: the LMS, the London and North Eastern Railway (LNER), the Southern Railway (SR), and the Great Western Railway (GWR). The LMS was made up of the following the following companies: the London and North Western (LNWR), the Lancashire and Yorkshire (L&YR), the Midland (MR), the North Staffordshire, the Caledonian, the Highland and Glasgow and the South Western. At this time it became the largest railway company in the world. Other smaller companies were included in July of that year.

How did this affect Sir Henry and what would be his role in the new company? Because of the size of the LMS resulting from all the companies which had constituted its formation, there were many senior engineers and managers available from which to appoint new senior positions. Indeed there were a number of former CMEs to be considered for the new Chief Mechanical Engineer post and it was obvious many would be disappointed and upset not to achieve this exalted position. In the end the board of the LMS appointed George Hughes, who had been CME of the LNWR and the L&YR when they had merged in 1922. The main reason for this decision was that they wished to avoid too strong an influence of the Midland Railway on the new company. This fact, together with Hughes's experience and seniority, gave him indisputable qualifications for the post. Henry was appointed Deputy CME, whilst still retaining the responsibility of running the Derby works. The appointment of Hughes, his old mentor and friend from his Horwich days, was considered by the board of the LMS to not only reduce Henry's disappointment, but would create a successful working relationship which would be essential in the early years of the LMS.

Here we witness another of Henry's honourable characteristics in that he not only accepted the position but immediately put his full energy and enthusiasm into the massive challenges of organising the new railway company. This would not have been without problems in coordinating and encouraging the many different factions of the old railways, each with its own cultures and traditions.

At Derby he commenced a programme to continue the production and development of the Midland locomotives to replace older types of engine. He also began feasibility studies to produce a 4-6-0 three cylinder locomotive based on the reliable 4-4-0 compound. Hughes decided that a 0-6-0T shunting locomotive was needed for the new company and delegated the design work to Henry at Derby, Hughes remaining at Horwich. The result, using the 1899 Johnson 0-6-0T as a basis, was the excellent and reliable locomotive which became known as the 'Jinty' of which 422 were built over the period 1924 to 1930.

He also carried out reviews of the Crewe works in order to improve efficiency of locomotive production and maintenance. As a result of this the Divisional Mechanical engineer at Crewe, H.P.M. Beames, was sent to America to study their methods of repair and production of locomotives. These studies showed how savings of 20% could be achieved and after due deliberation Henry introduced them into the Crewe works.

Photo 16: A restored 0-6-0T 'Jinty' Locomotive 47493 on 26th April 2010 (Richard J. Kyte)

These methods were communicated to the ARLE for discussions ending in visits to Crewe by other CMEs including Maunsell and Gresley, who later introduced them to their own companies.

When the LMS was formed in 1923 it incorporated many different types of locomotive into its system. Among these were the 4-4-0 class 4P compound express engines which had excellent performance records since their introduction in the early 1900s. However they were at least 14 years old and did not have any superheating, a subject on which Fowler was an expert. Therefore it was not surprising that Derby ordered 20 new compounds with superheating and other modifications. A further 30 were then ordered with new interchangeable boilers, higher working pressures and improved fireboxes. These engines were built between 1924 and 1932 and proved to be a first class asset for passenger work.

Photo 17: 4-4-0 Class 4 Express Passenger Engine No.1000 (Richard J. Kyte)

In 1922 Henry was elected as Vice President of the Institution of Mechanical Engineers and President of the Engineering Section of the British Association in 1923.

Henry still had fond memories of his childhood and early education in Evesham and spite of being so busy, he and Emma still found time to visit his family who were still in business in the town. No doubt he would have taken more than a passing glance at the LMS station and yards for which he had become responsible in his senior role in the new railway company. He would also have been interested in the new Grammar School in Victoria Avenue. In fact he wrote an article in the first edition of the *Henrician* in 1924 and instituted a prize to be awarded at each speech day; now known as the 'Sir Henry Fowler Memorial Prize for Mathematics'. He would have also agreed with the forthright principles of the headmaster Dr Samuel Rennie Haslehurst whose beliefs in the need for higher education were the same as his own. This fact is well established in his Presidential Address to the Institution of Mechanical Engineers a few years later.

In the first ever edition of the *Henrician* published for the Easter term of 1924, the Headmaster, Dr Haslehurst in his introduction, thanks both "Dr Hayes and Sir Henry Fowler for their kind interest and active help." He also refers to Sir Henry as a friend. Sir Henry's article is as follows:

My first day at Evesham Grammar School, September 1879

By Sir Henry Fowler, K.B.E., Wh. Ex.

I feel very proud that the Head has asked me to write a few words for the first number of the "Henrician" and I have chosen for my subject one which is still a very vivid recollection to me, and which I hope may be of interest to those who still go to the School. It must be remembered that I am by no means the oldest Scholar alive, and that the day I am speaking of is only the one on which the present foundation started. There are several scholars alive who went to the school which was closed after 1870, amongst whom are Dr. Horace Haynes and my father. I always think of the school as starting, as it undoubtedly did, in the early days of the monastery, and that the date on the building only refers to the refounding by Prince Henry.

Before 1870 the educational facilities in the town were slight, and consisted of the National Schools in Evesham and Bengeworth, the British School in Swan Lane, and Deacle's School — in that house in Bengeworth in which I believe John Wesley used to preach. Besides these were several private schools, some of which took small boys, the chief being Miss Hill's, at what is now Mr. E.G. Righton's house in High Street, to which many future "Henricians," including myself, went.

The Rev. Frederick W. Holland was Vicar of Evesham, at that time, and there must be many who, like myself, can never cease revering his memory for his work, and that of Mr. Herbert New and other public spirited men, which resulted in our getting a better education. The Rev. F.W. Holland became the first nominal headmaster, and took the Classics in Divinity. I shall always remember his genial smile, while he had that great gift of conversation, even with small boys, of making us realize that he was really and sincerely interested in us individually.

The day for us to go to the new school at Lanesfield came at last, some of us going with mixed feelings. There had been an examination for "foundation" scholars, and to my intense disappointment I had failed in this, and remember still the tears I shed then and the joy I had on obtaining second place in the Christmas examination, the first position being occupied, I believe, by Charlie Bird, much my senior. On the opening day someone had arranged for several of us to go together, and so we Bengeworth boys, Edgar and Harold Pittway from Northwick Terrace, with Alf Bayliss and myself, set off over the bridge. On the other side we picked up Harry Sturch at the corner of Mill Street, and I think "Woowey" Haines on the hill. I know that Edward and, I believe, George Wheatcroft, came from the "Crown" and were allowed to join our gang as being friends of mine. We were very conscious of being objects of interest to "most all Esam," and well we might be, for we wore new "mortar boards," brand new, with their corners all correct and square, and very different from what they became by the end of the term when we realised what an offensive weapon they were. I am afraid our hats restrained us when we were scoffed at by the boys from Greenhill, whom we met going to school on the Green, but we dealt with them faithfully later when the novelty of the hat, as well as its sharp corners, had worn off.

The school at Lanesfield had not yet been built, and our main classroom was the conservatory on the south side of the house, were some local wit said we could be suitably "forced." The Master in charge of the school was the Rev. Sealey Poole, who is now a Rector near Weymouth, and who, I have recently heard from Mrs. Poole, is *still intensely interested in football, although I am afraid it is "soccer" instead of the "rugger" he was an ornament to in Evesham. Our playing field was at the back of the school, and in spite of a slope was, I thought it was, an excellent one. We played rugby naturally, and one of my most cherished memories still is of having unexpectedly, but none the less effectually, collared the "Rev Sealy" in a first practice, in which many of the men from the town joined.*

In the school the two top boys were Barlett, who became, I believe, a Barrister, and Edgar Pittway, who qualified as a Doctor, and died some years ago. There was keen competition between these two, as later there was between Harry Sturch, who is a dispenser in a navel establishment, and Harold Pittway, whom I have not heard of for years. The latter was brilliant for his age, and when he graduated at Victoria University was the youngest B.A. in the country. I started in Form II, and am afraid went up to Form III and back again several times, until in some way I have never been able to understand, I got into the IVth and became third boy in the School, and as Pittway wanted to wait another year, and Sturch did not wish to take the Exhibition, I became the first Workman Exhibitioner, and the youngest student at Mason College, Birmingham.

This article clearly demonstrates Sir Henry as a very sincere modest man, with a sense of humour, who was proud of his school and his birthplace, and that he retained those feelings all his life. His reference to the Workman Exhibitioner was the Workman Scholarship which was funded by Mr Henry Workman, the well-known public benefactor, who was Mayor of Evesham for five years and began the actions to replace the old Evesham Bridge with the Workman Bridge which was named after him. This Scholarship was worth £30. The *Worcester Chronicle* carried the following news on 15th August 1885.

> "*The first Workman Scholarship funded by Mr. H. Workman awarded to H. Fowler son of Mr Fowler of Bengeworth. Value is £30 a year.*"

This scholarship could be said to be the financial start to Sir Henry's illustrious contribution to the world of engineering and science.

In the summer of that year the occasion of a family visit to Evesham was a sad event. On 1st July, his father Henry senior died aged 81. The following notice appeared in *The Evesham Journal* dated July 5th 1924 3rd edition:

> **Fowler.** *On July 1st at Abbey Gates, Evesham, Henry Fowler died aged 81 years.*

The family travelled from Spondon to attend the funeral at Evesham Cemetery and stayed for a few days with the rest of the family. The entry in *The Evesham Journal* dated July 12 1924 read:

> **Henry Fowler.** *Funeral took place at Evesham Cemetery conducted by the Rev. H.D. Hilliard and attended by Sir Henry Fowler and Mr Charles Fowler (sons).*

In August Sir Henry had attended conferences in Canada and on his way back he wrote a short letter to the Headmaster of the Grammar School indicating his continued interest in its history. The text of the letter is given:

> *Canadian Pacific*
> *S.S Montroyal*
> *Aug 25th 1924*

Dear Dr. Hazelhurst.

I have been attending the British Association at Toronto and I took the opportunity of calling on the Rev. Robbins, an old Evesham Grammar School boy. I found he left Evesham when he was 14, but was still interested in the old town. At Cleveland I saw one of my cousins Mr. W.F. Nash, who was with me at the Grammar School.

I am enclosing P/O and should be glad if you could arrange for the "Henrician" to be sent to them, including No.1 if in any way possible. If I have not sent sufficient I will forward balance.

I hope it will be possible for me to get to the Prize Distribution this year.

With kind regards,
Yours sincerely,
HY. FOWLER.

September saw his second son Eric pass the necessary entrance examinations to enable him to go to Oundle School where he became an excellent scholar and sportsman during his five years at the school.

During this time Hughes had been producing designs for larger locomotives of which he would have discussed with Henry. These included a 4-6-2 Pacific Express, a 2-6-0 Mixed Traffic and a 2-8-0 Heavy Freight engine.

The new LMSR Board under the chairmanship of Sir Guy Granet included a number of ex MR Directors and representatives of the accountancy profession. This combination allowed the old MR 'small engine' policy to be maintained in the new regime, a factor which proved to be a retrograde step. George Hughes (CME) held his newly created position for a relatively short time, deciding to retire in October 1925 and pursue his own horticultural interests which he continued for the next 20 years. Was the fact that he was relatively young to retire because (like his predecessor Deeley) of his frustration at the LMSR Boards negative attitude to change? Andrew Roden the author of many excellent books on railway history and contributing editor of *International Railway Journal*, together with a number of eminent railway engineers and historians, regarded the Board's decision to maintain the 'small engine policy' as short-sighted. The other railway companies competing with the LMSR recognized the future need for increased loads on both passenger and goods trains and encouraged the design of larger locomotives.

Sir Guy Granet immediately took action to restore the design office at Derby and to ensure that the transfer of this work from Horwich went smoothly and logically. Sir Henry was appointed CME of the LMSR but with the old MR policy still in place. As CME, Henry became responsible for all design, development and production of locomotives at Crewe, Derby, Horwich and St. Rollox including all steel works, foundries and rolling mills. These latter duties would have been of special interest as he was an expert in metallurgy. All design work and projects were moved to Derby and he began the organisation and development for the future, although still bounded by the LMS Board's policies.

In 1926 an important and far reaching appointment was made by the LMS Board. Sir Josiah Stamp an acknowledged and brilliant economist was appointed to sort out the management structure of the company. It seems ironical that one of his first observations was to question why most express trains from London to the North were double headers, whereas other railway companies used larger single locomotives. He did not receive a valid explanation for this from the Directors, (which must have caused a great deal of embarrassment in the LMS Board Room). Stamp then urged Henry to provide a locomotive which was powerful enough to meet this deficiency. There would be no doubt what Henry must have felt at this point bearing in mind his efforts and the efforts of his predecessors, Deeley and Hughes, to produce designs particularly for the compound Pacific which had been rejected by the Board for so long. However other events overtook any action and set the pattern for the future.

Comparison trials between LNER Pacific and GWR Castle Class locomotives had proved the GWR engine to be superior on express routes. From the actions taken in response, it would appear that the LMS Board realised that their negative small engine policy of locomotive power had been exposed. It was the first failing in management that Stamp had identified. In their obvious haste to be seen to be proactive they sought to bypass the CME. Sir Guy Granet sought the help of the GWR General Manager, Sir Felix Pole, who was a close friend, and arrangements were made for a Castle 4-6-0 to undertake trials between Euston and Carlisle. Again the result of these tests proved the excellent design of the Castle, which loaded between 450 and 500 tons had cleared Shap Fell without any banker assistance which the LMS locomotives had failed to do with similar loads. Immediately after the completion of the trials on the 20th November 1926 the Board directed Henry to produce 50 'improved Castles' to be ready for the next summer. This was a massive task and it was clear that if the normal design capabilities were used, the timescale would have been almost impossible. Henry needed all his expertise in engineering, organisational and management skills to be brought to bear on the project. However, he must have recognised the similarly to the tasks he so successfully accomplished when he first went to Farnborough.

The LMS Board again tried to side-line him and be seen to put themselves in a good light by requesting the GWR design offices at Swindon to provide them with drawings of the Castle class engines so that they could build similar locomotives. Swindon refused this request which must have been very embarrassing, particularly to Sir Guy Granet.

At this point Henry, although having been ignored by the Board, proved his stalwart character once again and went to see his old friend Richard Maunsell who was now the CME of the Southern Railway. Munsall had recently designed a locomotive of similar power to the GWR Castle Class: Class LN "Lord Nelson" which was proving a success on express trains. Henry obtained permission to use the design drawings to enable him to speed up development of a new locomotive meeting both the LMS Board's requirements and timescales. He instructed the Derby Chief Draughtsman to work with the Southern team to produce working drawings for production. Using all his expertise he negotiated a contract with the North British Railway Company (NBRC) to "design and build" a 4-6-0 3 cylinder express locomotive based on his specifications. His actions saved the Board further criticism and great credit must go to him for his demonstration of dignity in a situation where he must have been aggrieved in the manner in which he had been bypassed as CME.

The amount of work and management of this project was enormous and Henry worked endlessly with North British Locomotive Company (NBL) in the production of the first locomotive in July 1927. The new locomotives were designated as the 'Royal Scot' class and the first express passenger run was on the 26th September 1927, a non-stop journey from Euston to Carlisle. This event was greeted with much enthusiasm as a new advance in speed of travel on the railways. An article in *The Times* dated 22nd March 1933 refers to this event as 'Railway Rivalry' and described train speeds in history and famous runs from 1888 to 1933. This locomotive hauled a load of 420 tons, which consisted of 15 carriages, with great success and was testament to the quality of design and development which had been achieved over such a short timescale. Sir Henry was delighted in the performance and must have been enormously satisfied that his work with Maunsell had produced a locomotive similar to his earlier designs which had been rejected by the LMS Board. This locomotive condemned the 'small engine policy' to history, with the way forward to ever more powerful motive power.

Photo 18 shows 'Royal Scot' class No.6155 'The Lancer.' From this photograph it can be seen that the boiler design and general size and shape were similar to the Southern class 'Lord Nelson'.

However, there were a number of differences, for example the working pressures, number of cylinders and size of driving wheels. Fifty of these 'Royal Scot class were produced with new designs of bearings and with wheel couplings equally spaced giving equal axle loading, which was in contrast to the standard LMS six wheeled configuration. This locomotive soon replaced the smaller express engines on the London to Scotland routes and effectively ended the design of small locomotives.

This significant development poses the question: If Fowler's design for a 4-6-2 Pacific locomotive had not been rejected by the LMS Board, might the company have been the leading locomotive power some years ahead of their rivals? It is interesting to note that the power of the Royal Scot Class at a TE of 33,000 lbs was slightly more than the Britannia Class Pacific 4-6-2 designed by Robert Riddles in 1951. This perhaps puts into perspective the superior designs that Deeley, Hughes and Fowler had proposed all those years earlier.

Photo 18: 4-6-0 Royal Scot Class No.6155 'The Lancer' (H.C. Casserley)

At this time there was a need for a powerful medium sized tank engine. Fowler considered an earlier design by Hughes for a mixed traffic 2-6-4 tank engine and ordered the Derby draughtsman to produce a modified design. This resulted in the production of a very successful 2-6-4T locomotive capable of speeds up to 80 m.p.h. These were often used on London commuter routes and continued in service until 1966. A number of these locomotives were regularly used on the Birmingham to Ashchurch line and were seen daily at Evesham.

The workload at this time was very heavy and Henry had little time for other activities although he somehow managed to continue his support of the Bible classes (see Photo *26*), his work and interest in local events at Spondon, including his being a District Commissioner of Scouts.

Because of his workload, Anderson, as Superintendent of Motive Power at Derby, was delegated to negotiate with Beyer-Peacock, a large engineering and locomotive builder for the production of large mineral engines for hauling heavy coal trains from the mines at Toton to Brent. These loads had been hauled for many years by double headed class 4F 0-6-0 locomotives, which were slow and needed a great deal of maintenance due in no small measure to the massive loads they were handling. The result was a powerful 2-6-0:0-6-2 engine of which 33 were built from 1927 and remained in service until 1956. They did not perform as well as expected due mainly to the specifications given to Beyer-Peacock, who later designed and built a superior 2-6-2:2-6-2 design for overseas clients.

Although it was Anderson who specified the requirements to Beyer-Peacock, Fowler was CME but was not involved with the final specification, due to his very heavy workload. However he must have been disappointed with the running costs of these locomotives. They were used extensively on the Toton to Brent route, but they were occasionally employed hauling heavy loads from South Wales to the Midlands. *Photo 19* shows a Beyer-Garratt locomotive, tender first, hauling a heavy coal train. On one occasion due to Sunday maintenance work on the main line, two of these locomotives were diverted via the Ashchurch to Redditch branch line.

Photo 19: 2-6-0:0-2-6 Beyer- Garratt on a Toton to Brent coal train

Both locomotives stopped at Evesham to fill their water tanks and provided a unique spectacle to a few young train spotters who happened to be around. This event occurred in the mid 1950's maintenance or very rare disruption to mainline traffic did allow a few occasions for Fowler express locomotives to passing through Evesham.

For some time there had been a need for a mixed traffic locomotive and Fowler turned to the 2-6-0 (Hughes design) which had been partly constructed for this application. He made a number of modifications to the design and the first locomotive was completed in 1926. This proved to be an excellent design and the locomotives were used extensively throughout the LMS network. A total of 245 locomotives were built, the last being withdrawn in 1967. A photograph of one of this class is shown at LMS Evesham Station (*Photo 20*).

Photo 20: Hughes/Fowler 2-6-0 class 6P5F at Evesham 1956 (H. Casserley)

Later in the year the University of Birmingham awarded an Honorary Degree of LLD to Sir Henry, recognising an old student of the Mason Science College which later became the University's science faculty.

Chapter 8: The Demise of the Small Engine Policy

In 1927 the LMSR Board finally accepted that their small engine policy was finished and there followed a period of activity to redress the lack of suitable locomotive power available for a wide range of duties. One requirement that had become pressing was the need for a medium size tank engine for general duties in all areas of the LMS. Sir Henry directed Derby office (1926-1927) to produce a design to meet these requirements. The result was an excellent passenger tank engine suitable for local commuter routes as well as light freight. The locomotive was designated as a 2-6-4T Class 4P, with a tractive effort of 23,125 lbs. It was introduced in 1927 and a total of 125 were built. Many of these locomotives remained in service until 1966 and were a regular sight at Evesham, serving the Birmingham to Ashchurch route.

Sir Henry still displayed great physical and mental energy both in his work and outside activities. These included work for the Institutions of Mechanical Engineers, Locomotive Engineers and Civil Engineers as well as his interest in International bodies.

It was in 1847 that George Stephenson, designed and built the first public railway system between Stockton and Darlington. He was considered at the time to be the greatest mechanical engineer and was elected to be the first President of the Institution of Mechanical Engineers. Following his fine example, Sir Henry Fowler was elected to be the forty second President in 1927. His Presidential Address given to the Institution in October of that year is considered by many distinguished engineers to prove his status and high regard in the engineering world. His address illustrates many of his engineering principles were based on the work of George Stephenson.

In his address, Sir Henry referred to the brilliant work of George Stephenson and other engineers of that time and how many of his own engineering principles were based on their pioneering efforts. He admired their initiatives in producing first class engineering designs and solutions for example, Stephenson's locomotives, steam engines for pumps, and industrial machinery. All this was achieved with simple tools and machines prior to the use of more advanced machines which were later invented and developed.

He pointed out how his own engineering education at the Mason College in Birmingham and the enthusiasm of Professor Turner had given him a lifelong interest in metallurgy, a subject which he considered to be very important for engineers whose work depended so much on the use of metals. He continues by giving a sound description of the properties of metals, their characteristics and their use in different engineering applications such as boilers and load bearing vehicles. He concluded with support for education standards for young engineers, referring to the Institutes work with the Board of Education in introducing National Certificates and Diplomas which were to become the standard levels up to the present day. The full text of the address is reproduced in Appendix 3.

Following the address, votes of thanks were given by two past Presidents which illustrates the esteem and high regard in which Sir Henry's work and contribution to engineering was held. The extracts shown are reproduced with the kind permission of the Institution of Mechanical Engineers. The subjects and contents of the address suggested to many of his peers and later engineers just how much of his engineering talents, skills and knowledge had been lost to the LMSR by its negative management policies to Fowler's locomotive designs and his research for the development of larger and more powerful locomotives.

In the *Henrician* of 1928, the Headmaster, Dr Hazelhurst comments:

> *"The School congratulates Sir Henry Fowler K.B.E. LLD. On being elected to the Presidency of the Institution of Mechanical Engineers. It is noted that Sir Henry paid a tribute to the world famous Northumbrian pioneer of locomotion in his opening address. Of course we refer to the poor shepherd lad – as "Geordie Steve." Sir Henry has promised the School a photo of the engine "The Great Scot" and one of the First Grammar School Cricket match"*

Henry did not neglect his other interests, playing cricket for Spondon and writing under the pen name 'Bully Off' on the subject of hockey for the Derby Telegraph. He also continued his work as a District Commissioner of Scouts. Together with Emma he organised Sunday afternoon teas at Spondon Hall for apprentices and pupils, showing his interest in the life and careers of young people. He also organised functions for the elderly people of Spondon, supported local fetes and continued with bell ringing at the Church. He supported the church by becoming a member of a number of Diocesan Conferences and a delegate on the Church Assembly. Emma continued her involvement in the Women's Institute and other village activities as well as being a magistrate at Derby.

Although approaching 60 years of age, when many people having achieved most of their ambitions would consider taking life a little easier, this was not to be in Henry's case. Indeed the opposite was true and he continued to approach all demands on his time as he had done throughout his life. He is quoted as saying *"My worst enemy is time."* His contribution to engineering, science, education, national and international events as well as social welfare and local community support, continued at a pace.

PRESIDENT.

Sir Henry Fowler — John Kyte

Photo 21: Sir Henry (left) at Spondon Fete on 28th June 1934 (Spondon Historical Society)

As CME of the LMS his workload was increased by the demand for new locomotives both for passenger and freight. This was brought about by the deteriorating state of the railway systems after the First World War together with the expansion and the ever increasing public use of the railways. In 1928 he initiated the design of an updated Hughes Class 2P 4-4-0 of the Midland Railway. Changes included higher steam pressures and reduced diameter driving wheels. A total of 138 were built and they provided a good light load passenger locomotive with the lowest repair cost of any of the LMS types. This was a very successful engine, although it did not become as well known as the Royal Scot. They continued in service until the last were withdrawn in 1962. This was followed by the design of a 2-6-2T Light Passenger engine built specifically for the Moorgate London routes.

Throughout his career Henry had studied the science and technology of the properties of superheated steam. He applied this technology to an experimental design in an attempt to increase the thermal efficiency of a locomotive without increasing its mechanical size. He had hoped to apply this to the Royal Scot class as an economical way of increasing power. Using a German design of a high pressure boiler, a 4-6-0 locomotive was ordered in 1929 from the North British Locomotive Company. The locomotive was given the name 'Fury', a name that was originally carried by No. 6138 of the Royal Scot class. The boiler system consisted of a complicated triple pressure unit in which pressures were 1400, 900 and 250lbs per square inch. The firebox water tubes were pressurised at 1400lbs per square inch. Test runs were made in early 1930 in the Glasgow area. However on the 10th February a tragic and catastrophic failure of one of the firebox pressure tubes resulted in the death of a locomotive inspector and serious injury to an engineer. Following an enquiry the locomotive was returned to Derby were it remained until rebuilt by Stainer in 1935. Similar experimental locomotives using high pressure boilers in Canada and France were also later abandoned due to poor results.

The new enlightened approach by the LMS Board to more powerful engines meant that consideration was given to the design of a standard heavy mineral engine. At this time Sir Henry's attention was drawn again to the provision of powerful and efficient engines to haul heavy mineral trains. Although the Beyer-Garratts (Beyer, Peacock) had gone some way to solving the problems by the use of the smaller 0-6-0s, there was a need for a more powerful locomotive to fill this requirement. An old LNWR class 0-8-0 design was used as a basis for a new more efficient locomotive using an improved boiler, higher pressures, greater firebox capacity and other advanced mechanical improvements. This resulted in the 0-8-0 Class 7F Mineral Engine (*Photo 22*) which was introduced in 1929, a total of 175 being built. Its appearance was a typical Derby design with recognised Fowler features including a high running plate clear of the wheels avoiding the use of splasher plates, which created a deep buffer-beam at the front of the engine. These features gave an improved steam distribution system and a significant reduction in fuel usage.

Photo 22: 0-8-0 Class 7F Mineral Engine (H.C. Casserley)

Following the success of the Royal Scot locomotives, there still remained a need for an express passenger engine which could cover a wider route operation than the Royal Scot. Sir Henry and the Derby design team decided to combine the best engineering aspects of the ex-LNWR Claughton 4-6-0, 4 cylinder express locomotives with the basic Royal Scot locomotives. To achieve this objective, two Claughtons were withdrawn from service and rebuilt to the new designs. The extensive running tests on the resulting 3-cylinder locomotives proved them to be superior with much lower running costs. Based on these trails the LMS Board gave the go ahead for 50 more locomotives to be built. These were constructed over four years from 1930 to 1934. Their size, appearance and speeds being so close to the Royal Scot class, led to them being referred to as 'Baby Scots'. However they were to become designated as the 'Patriot' class, and proved to be excellent express passenger engine and ran until 1965 (*Photo 23*) .

In 1943 several of the later built locomotives were given names, but probably due to the war, never carried a nameplate. Engine No

45550 was named Sir Henry Fowler. None of this class of locomotive was preserved, but readers will be interested to note that a 'new' Patriot locomotive, based on the original design drawings is being constructed by the Llangollen Railway Society and is to be named 'The Unknown Warrior' No.45551.

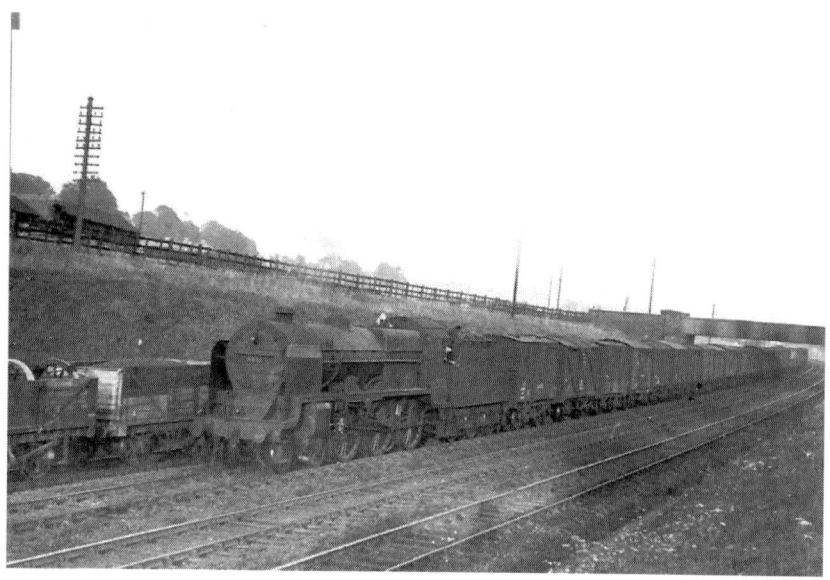

Photo 23: 4-6-0 Patriot Class No. 45532 'Illustrious' Northchurch (Aug. 1947)

In June 1929 the University of Manchester conferred the Honorary Degree of Doctor of Science on Sir Henry. This was recognition of the contribution to mechanical engineering and the research and development of locomotive power.

Professor Alexander who presented the degree outlined the achievements of Sir Henry by saying:

> *"He has been the parent of many standard types of locomotives, a progeny of the beautiful and prodigious monsters, of which the last and most prodigious was the 'Royal Scot'. Innumerable medals or prizes have acknowledged the value of his increasing contributions to engineering science, and with all the engrossing duties of his great*

> *domestic office he has contrived to keep abreast of scientific and practical abroad and in America, and adapt them to our advantage.*

Above all he is distinguished by his constant effort through personal intercourse to excite a spirit akin to his own love of their profession among young engineers, for whom he is a never-failing fountain of enthusiasm and experience distributed through the conduits of inexhaustible speech."

This tribute illustrates that Sir Henry had achieved the recognition of the engineering and academic world. It also dismisses any doubts about the success of the Royal Scot locomotive.

Professor Alexander also pointed out the simpler but endearing character of Sir Henry in relation to engineering in everyday life:

> *"Lest of all would I forget that his concern with greater mechanisms had not blunted his passion for riding the humble, familiar bicycle"*

Photo 24: The original signed photograph of the 'Royal Scot' presented to Prince Henry's Grammar School by Sir Henry, in 1928.

The image of the signed photograph of the 'Royal Scot' is reproduced by the kind permission of Mr Bernard Roberts, Head teacher of Prince Henry's High School. The locomotive is in its grey works paint and still at the North British Railway Company Works.

This photograph is preserved in the library of Prince Henry's High School, Evesham.

Chapter 9: Leaving the Chief Mechanical Engineer's Chair

In 1930 Sir Henry was approaching his sixtieth year and the President of the LMSR Sir Josiah Stamp, was looking to the future of the railway company. Among his thoughts was a change in the CME's department to introduce new technology in locomotive design. The previous year Sir Josiah had persuaded Sir Harold Hartley, a Fellow of the Royal Society and of Balliol College Oxford, to become Vice President and Director of Scientific Research. Sir Harold had no previous experience of the railway industry or mechanical engineering and obviously required assistance. This was to prove an ideal diplomatic opportunity to convince Sir Henry that his experience in research could be used in the post of Assistant to the Vice President of Scientific Research.

Although some people thought this was a step down from CME, Sir Henry weighed up many aspects of the new post in a typical positive way. Not only did it afford him the chance to combine his engineering talents with his interest of research projects in mechanical engineering and metallurgy, but it also allowed him more time to devote to the Institutions, which were all based in London. An additional advantage, although a sad one, was that Emma was in poor health and Sir Henry could spend more time attending to her welfare.

As he had always done, he took on the new challenge immediately and began the task of building a centre at Derby which would provide facilities for new research and technology. The departments he set up included chemical and paint laboratories, engineering and metallurgy; a particular interest which he had studied from his early days at the Mason College.

Being a member of the Permanent Commission to the International Congress he contributed papers for discussions and in

1930 he undertook research with George Ellison, the Chief Civil Engineer of the Southern Railway on the static and dynamic stress in railway bridges. This illustrates the wide range of Sir Henry's knowledge in both research and engineering, which was now known worldwide. It is interesting to note that the appointment of William Stainer as the CME of the LMSR in 1931 by Sir Harold Hartley, was based on the opinion of Sir Henry who considered that this was a positive step forward for the company.

While undertaking this new and important work his energy and enthusiasm for outside interests was as strong as ever. He even found time to stand as an Independent in 1931, for a seat on Derbyshire County Council. However, on this occasion he was unsuccessful, losing by 144 votes. A short time later he and Emma came to Evesham on an annual visit to his parents' graves and stayed with his younger brother Charles, who still ran the family furniture business in High Street. During the rest of that year he attended conferences in Zurich and Paris.

In 1932 Sir Henry's research work was recognised by his appointment as one of three special reporters to the International Railway Congress Association whose task was to investigate "Methods to be used to increase the mileage run by locomotives between two repairs, including lifting." They were asked to report their findings at an IRC meeting in Cairo.

Although he was still very busy with all his research and engineering projects, concern about Emma was leading him to think of retirement. However he visited Germany to assess the development of locomotive technology, particularly diesel power in relation to experiments that he was overseeing at Derby. In the same year he was elected President of the Institute of Metals, which recognised the research and contribution to metallurgy which he had undertaken during his career.

This honour was followed by probably the most prestigious honour, that of Life Membership of the Institution of Mechanical Engineers, an award made to only a few distinguished engineers.

Late in 1932 he resigned from the LMSR, to enable him to continue his Chairmanship of the Ministry of Transport, but really one may surmise, to take care of his beloved Emma.

He also handed over his research projects to his principal assistants to enable him to concentrate on the preparation of the report for the 1933 International Railway Congress in Cairo . This was the study in which he had participated on the locomotive milage between overhauls, a subject in which he had always been interested since the early days at Horwich. The trip was unaccompanied as Emma's health preventing her travelling abroad.

Following the Congress, in the company of other scientists and renowned engineers, he set out on a trip to see more of Egypt and Palestine. This must have been a wonderful expereance for he was to witness the people, cultures, traditions and countries on which his Christian faith had been founded.

A few days after he returned from Egypt he and Emma attended an Institution of Metals dinner in London, where they stayed at the St Pancras Hotel.

By now he had reduced his committments allowing more time to pursue other interests, including his lifetime love of cricket. Together with Emma, he made a number of visits to the Derbyshire Cricket Club and relaxed while enjoying the county games.

Meanwhile back at the LMSR, William Stainer, the CME was scrapping many of the old locomotives and replacing them with new designs, reflecting the developments which had been made over the previous decades, some to which Sir Henry had contributed.

It is interesting to note that Stainer designed two 'Pacifics' 4-6-2s which bore similar features to the 'Pacific' compound engine that Sir Henry had proposed some eight years earlier. Stainer also retained the most successful 'Royal Scot' and 'Patriot' Class locomotives, together with the reliable 0-6-0 freight engine which were all Fowler locomotives.

Many of the design features of the 'Royal Scot' and 'Patriot' classes were also incorporated into Stainers successful 'Jubilee'class locomotive This action supports the excellence of Sir Henry's design of locomotives at the time when he was being frustrated by the small engine policy.

About this time his son Eric graduated from Clare College, Cambridge and it must have been a great pleasure that both Sir Henry and Lady Emma could attend the ceremony.

Photo 25: Sir Henry and Lady Fowler with Eric at his Graduation from Clare College Cambridge (Spondon Historical Society)

Chapter 10: Journey's End

In 1934 Eric, who after leaving Cambridge had joined the police force to gain some experience of the law, gained a place in Gray's Inn to enable him to complete his studies for the Bar. Sir Henry who was still quite active attended a conference in September of the British Association at Aberdeen, taking part in debates and discussions with his usual enthusiasm and energy both as a speaker and Chairman.

Fate however intervened and he collapsed and became unwell. The doctor who attended him recommended that he should return home immediately and to take a complete rest. Sir Josiah Stamp, the Chairman of the LMSR who was at the conference, assumed immediate charge of Sir Henry and ensured that he travelled with a nurse on an express train to Crewe. From there a special train was arranged to continue his journey back to Derby where an ambulance was waiting to take him straight to Spondon. Sir Henry's own doctor confirmed that he was exhausted and very ill and needed immediate rest with all engagements cancelled.

This must have been a blow to him, for all his life his robust health and physique had enabled him to achieve so much. However, worse was to follow with the death of Emma on 1st November, her 63rd birthday.

It would be impossible to imagine the effect this had on Sir Henry, for it was 42 years before, on Emma's 21st birthday, that he had asked her to become his wife. His daughter Dorothea stayed at Spondon to care for him and share his grief, but his health was so poor that he was unable to attend Emma's funeral. It took some time before he was well enough to resume his work, but he was never going to be the same outgoing, energetic man after these tragic few months.

Towards the end of the year his son Eric became engaged to Gwendoline May Bignall, whom he had met the previous year and this helped to bring some cheer back into Sir Henry's life.

The family persuaded him to spend some time away from Spondon. Taking their advice he departed on a P&O cruise to Australia, which called at Marseilles, Port Said, Aden, Bombay, Colombo and Freemantle. He enjoyed the relaxed time on the cruise and wrote letters to the family describing the various places he visited. He spent Christmas in Sydney and soon became known to the Bishop, after attending services at the Cathedral and had the pleasure of being entertained to supper at Bishopscourt the official home of the Bishop of Sydney.

Following his stay in Australia he travelled to New Zealand for a further two weeks tour before returning home in much better health and with some of the old determination to resume his many interests. Among these included his old Bible Class where in 1935 a reunion was held. Many of those attending, having survived the First World War.

Photo 26: Sir Henry (centre) at the Bible Class Reunion 1935 (Spondon Historical Society)

Photo 27: Sir Henry (centre back row) at OAP Tea Party 1934

Photographs *26* and *27* show Sir Henry attending some local events at Spondon, illustrating the interest and support he gave willingly to the local community which he so loved. Photographs supplied generously by Spondon Historical Society.

Early in 1935 he returned to the Ministry of Transport and the Committee of Noise Prevention, a subject in which he had been interested for many years. When Eric and Gwen announced the date they planned to get married Sir Henry insisted that he made all the arrangements for a splendid celebration of the occasion. The wedding took place at Spondon Parish Church, followed by a grand reception in a marquee in the grounds of Spondon Hall. This event, on the 16th April 1936 was to be a final social event in Sir Henry's life, for by this time his health was deteriorating and was of great concern to his family and friends.

In 1937 Eric, who had completed his studies in law, was called to the Bar and practiced as a barrister until the outbreak of the war. He immediately joined the RAF and served in Bomber Command as a navigator, flying on raids over Germany. As the year progressed Sir Henry suffered a number of mini-strokes and his health deteriorated rapidly. He needed a full time nurse to be at Spondon Hall and was at times confined to a wheelchair. All his outside duties had ceased and he was unable to attend church and the bell ringing he so loved.

In January 1938 he handed over the Captaincy of the Bell ringers to George Wright his friend and fellow bell ringer. In his note to George he expressed his hope that he would soon be able to help again. This, one suspects, was a forlorn hope. Indeed he suffered another stroke shortly afterwards. However, even at this stage he still managed to write short notes to friends in Spondon and on one occasion arranged for flowers to be sent to a villager who had been ill, with a short note wishing her well again.

Early in October his condition became critical and on Sunday 16th October Sir Henry passed away at Spondon Hall. *The Times* newspaper published the following under 'Deaths'; dated 18th October 1938:

> *On Oct 16 at Spondon Hall Derbyshire,*
> *Sir Henry Fowler, aged 68.*
> *Funeral at St. Werburgh's Spondon 2.30 pm. tomorrow (Wednesday).*
> *No flowers by his request.*

The funeral service was conducted by the vicar and the curate of Spondon: the Revs H.C. Brocklehurst and C. Herve, who were assisted by the Rev. J.E. Dallimore, a lifelong friend of Sir Henry. Many of the villagers and close friends were in attendance to express their sorrow at losing such a beloved member of their community.

The coffin, of English Oak, bore the inscription: "Henry Fowler, at rest, 16 October 1938, aged 68." On 18th October, *The Times* listed many of the people present at the funeral service which clearly shows the influence Sir Henry had on the engineering world.

Among those present were:

Mr. Henry Fowler and Mr. G.E. Fowler (sons). Mr Alec Fowler and Mr. Charles Fowler (brothers). Mr. J Bomford (brother in law), and Mr. C. Bomford, Mr. T.M. Herbert (representing Sir Harold Hartley, vice–president LMS Railway Company), Major G.S. Bellamy (representing Mr. W.A. Stainer, Chief Mechanical Engineer, Euston), Mr. T.F. Coleman. (Technical Assistant and Chief Draughtsman, Locomotive Drawing Office Derby), Mr. J. Rankin (Chief Mechanical Engineers Department Crewe, Mr. J. Clayton, (Assistant Mechanical Engineer), also representing Sir H. Nigel Gresley, Mr. O. Bullard and Mr G. Szlumper). Captain J.A.E. Drury-Lowe, Dr. T. Swinden, Professor C.H. Bullerd (Institution of Mechanical Engineers and Nottingham University). Mr A.J. Smout. (Institute of Metals). Mr Neville Gretton, Lieutenant-Colonel J.W. Watkins (representing Lieutenant-Colonel J.H. Fellows, former vice-president of the L.M.S Railway Company.

Following the service Dorothea, Henry and Eric together with their uncles Alec and Charles travelled to Nottingham Road Cemetery, Derby, for the burial. Sir Henry was laid to rest with Emma and their baby son Geoffrey, aged 7 months, who had died 35 years earlier. The simple headstone on the family grave has the following inscription:

>
> Loving memory of
> EMMIE NEEDHAM FOWLER
> Loving wife of
> HENRY FOWLER
> BORN Nov 1ST 1872
> DIED ON HER BIRTHDAY 1934
>
> AND OF HER HUSBAND
> HENRY FOWLER
> WHO DIED Oct 16th 1938
> AGED 68

The Rev. H.C. Brocklehurst gave the obituary at the funeral in which he expressed the great loss to the Church, the local community and the Engineering world, in the passing of Sir Henry. He also referred to the special interest Sir Henry had in the churchyard:

> *"Coming from a part of the country where they take great pride in their Churchyards it was great satisfaction when, after expenditure of much labour, it was, at last, possible to mow the grass and keep it tidy..."*

In 1941, Eric was awarded the Distinguished Flying Cross for outstanding service in Bomber Command. Had he been alive, his father, although no doubt sad that war had come again, would have would have been proud of his son's service to his county.

Tributes from the engineering, academic and associated professions, as well as local communities and newspapers praising Sir Henry's contributions to many walks of life, were received following his death. He never forgot Evesham and visited when he could, staying with his brother, meeting local people he knew and seeing the town which he knew so well from his early days. He maintained a great interest in Prince Henry's Grammar School and attended a number of events when time allowed. He always acknowledged his early education and the career direction he was encouraged to take by the teachers at the school.

The exhibition and the Sir Henry Fowler Room goes some way to acknowledging the contribution that a son of Evesham and Old Henrician, made to the later years of the Industrial Revolution, the engineering world and to the education of later generations.

There can be no doubt the esteem in which he was held and a tribute to the high principles of his Christian faith, which had originated with his family in Evesham.

Chapter 11: Vale Connections

It would be a pity not to bring to the reader's attention to a few examples of Sir Henry Fowler's contribution to railway transport in the Vale of Evesham.

From a local history point of view the LMS was a branch line running from Birmingham New Street to Ashchurch. The original plans were for it to have been an alternative route to the Gloucester to Birmingham line, which includes the Lickey incline. Due to economic restrictions and the problem of tunnelling at Redditch, the line was downgraded to single working between Redditch and Evesham. This meant that apart from a few occasions, larger express locomotives which were designed by Sir Henry were not seen in Evesham. However to complete the picture of his life and work the following short accounts are given as a record.

Photo 28: Fowler 2-6-4T Evesham to Birmingham at Broom Junction (2nd May 1947)

Photo 29: Hughes/Fowler 2-6-0 Class 6P5F New Street to Ashchurch (26th Sept 1959)

Photo 30: Fowler 2-6-4T, 9.40 a.m. Ashchurch to New Street, at Beckford (24th April 1958)

Photo 31: Fowler 0-6-0 Class 4F No.44422 at Wansford, Nene Valley Railway (Richard J. Kyte)

The 0-6-0 Class 3F and 4F were excellent locomotives and proved to be first class workhorse for the Midland Railway and later the LMS. They were used mainly for heavy goods trains and were seen at Evesham hauling fruit and vegetable loads to the North and to Scotland, and goods from Birmingham to Bristol. Here can be seen a direct link to the man who was born in Port Street, Evesham, educated at the Grammar School, who probably would have known many of the growers in the Vale and whose engineering brilliance, provided some of the locomotives that assisted the growth of the agricultural industry.

The photograph of No 4169 passing through the Bengeworth Station is of particular interest as Sir Henry was born in Bengeworth (which was the part of Evesham). Because of their design and driving wheel layout, they had a tendency to 'wobble' and in some parts of the country they were known as 'Ducks'.

Photo 32. Fowler 0-6-0 Class 4F passing Bengeworth Station (which was in Hampton) (Middleton Press)

In Evesham the LMS line ran on the High Street side of the Railway Hotel and eastward. There was a steep incline for about 400 yards to enable the line to cross above the GWR line. At the point where the two lines converged, the LMS line turned about 70 degrees to the North. This was a difficult piece of track for it meant that a loaded train say 300 tons plus, needed a powerful start from the station to gain sufficient momentum to overcome the incline and the sharp bend.

At night, when there were a number of trains including goods from Bristol, it was fairly common for the locomotive to fail to gain the necessary speed to successfully climb the incline. Bear in mind that because of the bend, the locomotive was handicapped by speed restrictions. Many drivers set the cut-off high giving more steam into the cylinders, and at the same time trying to open the regulator with a steady hand, only to be defeated by wheel slip. This had the effect of drawing the fire. The sight was spectacular at night because the hot flames from the firebox and the carryover of burning cinders were blasted from the chimney, lighting up the sky. Consequently, the steam pressure was dramatically lowered and the fireman had to work hard to feed coal into the firebox and operate the water injectors to make good the lost pressure. Sometimes, after a number of restarts on the incline had failed, the only course of action was to reverse the train back into the station and try to start the climb again. The tight bend also caused a great deal of friction on the flanges of the driving wheels on the 0-6-0's due to them not having a leading bogie wheel truck, resulted in great deal of noise generated as the locomotives rounded the curve of the track. This friction over time would cause wear on the wheel flanges and rails.

Living near the railway for some years I recall seeing these locomotives leaving for the North and some of the problems their crews had to deal with, on leaving Evesham station.

Appendix 1: Extracts from *Times* obituary

Extracts from *The Times* obituary:

SIR HENRY FOWLER

LOCOMOTIVE DESIGNER

Sir Henry Fowler, DSc., the locomotive designer who was responsible for L.M.S. Royal Scot engines, died at Spondon Hall, Derbyshire, on Sunday night at the age of 68. Henry Fowler was born in Evesham on July 29 1870, and after going to school in his native town, attended the Mason Science College, the forerunner of the University of Birmingham… he was responsible for the design of various locomotives, including the "Royal Scots" and the high-pressure engine "Fury", and he also carried out a reorganization of the railway's locomotive repair shops, with a result that the number of locomotives under repair was greatly reduced and the smaller stock sufficed the needs of traffic… In 1917 he was created C.B.E and in 1918 was advanced to K.B.E. A frequent contributor of papers to the Institutions of Civil and Mechanical Engineers and other technical societies, he occupied the presidential chair of number of them… In 1895 he married Emmie Needham, daughter of the late Mr. Philip Smith. She died in 1934. There were two sons and a daughter of the marriage.

Many other obituaries were written including one from The Executive Committee of The International Railway Congress Association which praised his great contribution to engineering and to his ceaseless activity and cheerful disposition which was held in high esteem by his colleagues of the Permanent Commission.

Appendix 2: Presidential chairs & positions held

PRESIDENTIAL CHAIRS
University of Birmingham Engineering Society (1912-14)
The Institution of Locomotive Engineers (1912-14)
The Institution of Automobile Engineers (1920-21)
The Institution of Locomotive Inspectors and Firemen (1921-23)
The Institution of Mechanical Engineers (1927)
The Institute of Metals (1932)
The Engineering Section of the British Association (1923)

POSITIONS HELD
Member of the Council of the Institution of Civil Engineers. Paper read before the institution gained the Miller Prize, the Telford Premium, the Watt Medal and the Webb Prize.
Member of the Institute of Transport. Awarded Railway Engineering Gold Medal (1929-1930)
Assistant General Secretary of the Permanent Commission of the International Railway Congress Association, London (1925), Madrid (1930) and Cairo (1933)
He held the honorary degree of LL.D from the University of Birmingham, and a D.Sc. from the University of Manchester.
Boards of Management of Derby Royal Infirmary and Nightingale Nursing Home
Derby Borough Council Education Committee
Justice of Peace on Derby bench
Vice-President of the Henrician Union

Appendix 3: Presidential Address to the Institution of Mechanical Engineers 1927

Sir Henry Fowler wrote many papers on engineering and science subjects and references can be found on the internet. The papers were presented to the various professional institutes which began to be formed in the late 17th century. Three very important papers he wrote were given as his presidential addresses to the Institutions of Locomotive Engineers, Automobile Engineers and Mechanical Engineers respectively. These three Intuitions were amalgamated at various times to become the foremost mechanical engineering body in Britain and overseas. To become the President of The Institution of Mechanical Engineers and later elected a life member is an honour given to only a few of outstanding engineers.

Although the address is of a technical nature it should be of interest to students of engineering, local engineering enthusiasts and historians as it illustrates the achievements of the son of an Evesham family who was born in Port Street, educated at Prince Henry's Grammar School and went on to achieve the highest level in the mechanical engineering world.

Sir Henry Fowler's Presidential Address to the Institution of Mechanical Engineers 1927.

ADDRESS BY THE PRESIDENT,

Sir HENRY FOWLER, K.B.E., LL.D.

To be elected to the Chair once occupied by George Stephenson is an honour that every engineer, and especially every railway engineer, must covet, and I appreciate very deeply your having conferred this honour on me.

Not only railway engineering, but all branches of our profession have changed greatly since Stephenson occupied this Chair. His great work was so to improve the mechanical details of the steam-locomotive that it became the practical machine which revolutionized means of transport and did so much to advance the civilization of the world. There have been many great changes in the modes of life of the world, but none so far-reaching and rapid as that due to railway transport, and in no case has posterity singled out so unanimously the one man chiefly responsible for it. We do not perhaps realize as often as we should the difficulties that had to be surmounted in the mechanical engineering side of Stephenson's work, and it would be interesting if we could reconstruct the condition of mechanical engineering in those early days, so as to compare it with conditions at the present day. This is, however, not an easy matter when the diversity of our work is borne in mind; the very definition of mechanical engineering presents difficulties to-day, and it would be a great gain if we had a definition similar to that by which Telford differentiated between civil and military engineering. But we may say that in our branch of the great profession which adapts the forces of nature to the use of man, we are concerned with that which makes use of mechanisms of any form to achieve our object, and which deals with their design, manufacture, and operation. These mechanisms may vary from simple types, such as a lever, or a means of rotation, to the very elaborate forms used in automatic machines of complex structure, which require an expert to follow the functions of their apparently numberless parts.

Long before the foundation of our Institution various astronomical and other instruments of intricate and beautiful design had been made, but the appliances in ordinary use eighty years ago were very simple and, from our present point of view, crude. Though it would be so difficult to describe the actual state of mechanical engineering, as defined above, when George Stephenson was our President, in the short time I wish to devote to this part of my subject, the few points I mention may enable you to visualize it for yourselves. In the first place, the general machine-tools of the engineer's shop were few in number, although most of the simple types of machine which we use to-day had been invented and were being developed. It was, in fact, the period of the great pioneers of the machine-tool industty. Only a few years before, Maudslay had died, and Clement lived until 1844. Working in the development of the industry were Nasmyth, Roberts, Fox of Derby, and the greatest of all these machinists, our Past-President, Joseph Whitworth, whose Address in the eighth year of the Institution dealt with defects in iron, Bessemer's invention in steel manufacture, measurement, and increased production. He will live in our memories not only as one to whom so many of us are personally indebted for his interest in education, but for those wonderful general-purpose lathes of such good workmanship and design that many were to be found in jobbing engineering shops not many years ago. These, however, like the drills, planing machines, shaping machines, and slotting machines, which had just come into practical use, were simple in design, and according to our present ideas of production, slow in operation. Their slowness would probably impress us most, for they were dependent on cutting tools of plain carbon-steel, and we should find the design restricted by the general use of wrought and cast iron.

In spite of these limitations, however, the work produced was extremely good. At Swannington, at the end of the Leicester and Swannington Railway which was constructed in 1832 by George Stephenson, there is an incline of 1 in 17, up which coal was drawn in early days from a pit at the bottom, by means of a rope or chain. The haulage was performed by a horizontal engine with a piston-valve, fitted with "gab" valve-gear and installed in 1833 at the top of the incline. At the present time the same engine is employed about once a fortnight to lower coal to a drainage pump at the bottom of the incline, and to draw up the empty wagons. Until electric power is available I see no reason why the engine should not continue to operate as an economical and commercial proposition, and I can say that it will be a long time before it needs extensive repairs. It is interesting to note that the first automatic lathe was invented by Christopher M. Spencer at Amherst, Mass., U.S.A., in 1874.

Ideas we sometimes regard as new were passing through the minds of engineers in those early days. I will mention an example which is of particular interest at the present time. In 1848, Dr. Pole translated, from the German, Alban's book on a high-pressure boiler, which was, in fact, an interesting and early type of water-tube boiler. Alban held that boiler pressures should not be less than 8 to 10 atmospheres, and mentioned in an almost casual way that he had worked an engine with steam at a pressure of 1,000 lb. per sq. in. He said, "I firmly believe that these engines of great pressure would have produced good results." He found, however, that the steam generator was not perfect.

I have always been impressed by the fact that George Stephenson seemed to be not only conversant with, but an expert on all that was known and of interest concerning mechanical engineering in his day. The present time is naturally one of specialization, and even the ordinary course of three or four years at our Universities only covers a small part of the theoretical knowledge of our profession. I have been much struck with this, for in the course I took in mechanical engineering at Mason College, Birmingham, in 1885–7, I attended classes in metallurgy amongst other subjects, and had instilled into me an appreciation and devotion to this side of our work which I am thankful to say I have never lost. This, however, may have been largely due to the enthusiasm which Professor T. Turner seemed able to impart to those who were fortunate enough to be his students. But I was impressed a few years ago by the fact that graduates with good honours degrees of various Universities who came for their practical training to the works of which I have control, had little knowledge of metallurgy, which is surely one of the essential matters that should be understood by everyone who deals as we do with metals, their properties, and the effect of heat and fluids on them. This is only one instance that shows how impossible it is at the present day to cover completely, even with intensive study, the many branches of knowledge of our profession. We are expected to have a working acquaintance with many sides of science which have a distinct and important bearing on our work, and we may therefore truly say that progress in mechanical engineering is and has been, to a large extent, dependent on advances made in various other sciences.

Dr. Coker reminded me the other day that it has been said that the physics of to-day becomes the engineering of to-morrow. Sir James Henderson, when dealing with this point in his Presidential Address to the Engineering Section of the British Association at Leeds on 1st September, said, "This is a natural development since the engineer is more concerned than the physicist with the practical application of physical discoveries. But the converse is frequently true, for many physical discoveries and inventions arise in difficulties encountered by the engineer." Much of the work done in the furtherance of such science is as dependent on mechanical engineering, as we are so often on the results. It is on this interdependence of various sciences that I would now like to speak, and to endeavour to show how progress has been made thereby in the past eighty years, particularly in the materials we use.

Probably nearly everyone who has started to investigate a subject which appears wholly novel, finally agrees with the old philosopher who before the Christian era remarked that "there is no new thing under the sun." * Probably, too, they would agree with him when he went on to say :—

> "Is there anything whereof it may be said,
> See, this is new ?
> It hath been already of old time, which was before us.
> There is no remembrance of former things."

We are concerned chiefly with the development of discoveries and ideas on commercial lines for the use of Man, and for this development we are largely dependent on a thorough knowledge of the principles and conditions of the materials and mechanisms with which we deal.

Not because I am specially interested in the subject would I first of all like to speak of metallurgy, but because I think it will be agreed that it has probably played as great, if not a greater, part than any other in this development. Indeed we are apt sometimes to forget how essentially metals, and the physical state in which we are able to use them, dominate our work. Our whole profession is dependent on them, and although many ingenious contrivances have been made from wood and stone, mechanical engineering only commenced when metals became available for our use. This has

---

* Eccles. chap. i, verse 10.

undoubtedly effected a great change in civilization, for the various metals can now be obtained in quantity and at a reasonable price, whereas the knowledge of metals was very limited at the commencement of the period I am dealing with, and production was on what we now consider quite a small scale.

It will be remembered that the growth of railways seemed likely to be held up about the year 1850 owing to the inability of the production of iron rails to cope with the demand, and I believe the same can be said of shipbuilding, the situation only being relieved when Bessemer invented his process of steel manufacture. At the time when the "Rocket" was being built, not only was there no large commercial production of metals and alloys of the quality and type which we look upon as commonplace to-day, but the actual production was, to our present-day ideas, infinitesimally small. Of the basic material, cast iron, the whole amount produced in the world in 1850 was only $4\frac{1}{2}$ million tons; in 1926 this had grown to over 77 million tons. The amount of steel did not reach half a million tons per annum until 1870, whilst in 1926 it had reached over 90 million tons.

The "Rocket" was produced from ordinary cast and wrought iron, and a small amount of brass. Compare this small number of metals with the varied and complex quantities used in the construction of such a simple machine as a locomotive to-day! We must remember that the constituents of the three metals mentioned were not then properly understood nor were they sub-divided as they are now. Recently I have been standardizing the materials used on the 10,000 locomotives of the railway on which I am engaged, and I find that it is necessary to provide specifications for :—

$32\begin{cases}\text{Forged and Wrought Steels.} \\ \text{Cast Steels.}\end{cases}$
4 Wrought Irons.
3 Malleable and Cast Irons.
12 Brasses and Bronzes.
4 Other Metals.

Metals in which the tensile properties are the same, but which vary in method of manufacture or in chemical analysis, are counted as separate materials. Certain small requirements, such as special steel for the scoops of the pick-up apparatus, etc., are included.

It may also interest some members to know that the British Engineering Standards Association, on the basis stated above, legislate for well over 100 different classes of steel. This number seems large, and many may think it unnecessarily so, but I feel that if the total be analysed, they will be found to be all necessary for the general and complex work covered, especially if the aim of using materials which will combine safety and efficiency with the least possible cost is borne in mind.

Eighty years ago, as has been stated before, the world was approaching a crisis in the manufacture of iron and steel, and was about to enter what has been called the third great period of metallurgical progress, which was to help to change the civilization of the world. In the first period, from primitive times to the fourteenth century, iron and steel had been produced by deoxidizing the ore. This was followed by the indirect method of first producing a carbonized iron or cast iron, and then removing the superfluous carbon by somewhat tortuous methods at fairly low temperatures. Then came the Bessemer process in 1856, followed by the Siemens and Siemens-Martin processes, all dependent (like, in fact, Huntsman's production of steel in small quantities in a crucible) on a temperature which was sufficiently high to render the resulting product fluid enough to allow it to free itself from slag, etc. The time was ripe for this further advance, for as I have mentioned the very extension of railways and shipping was being retarded by the difficulty of obtaining sufficient wrought iron for rails, plates, etc. The same difficulties would have occurred with other manufactures, and it is interesting to note that before the first steel rails were laid in Crewe Station in 1861, a steel boiler had been built by Mr. Daniel Adamson in 1858. Not until 1867, however, was steel used for fireboxes fitted to locomotive boilers on the Lancashire and Yorkshire Railway, and such material was not used for a complete locomotive boiler at Crewe until 1868.

It may be that Bessemer was not in the full sense of the term a metallurgist, but he was undoubtedly a scientific man, and it was his capacity for using " ordered knowledge of natural phenomena and of the relation between them " (W. C. D. Whetham) that enabled him to get over his early difficulties. Siemens and the brothers Martin were metallurgists of standing, and it may be said that it was the work of these and other men at the same period which gave us that abundance of steel that once for all made the question of *quantity* one which need not be considered any longer. We are perhaps apt to forget that more than once in the history of industry the difficulties of actual supply have been a predominating factor in the progress of the world. Another well-known instance is that period in the middle of the eighteenth century, when the eating up of the forests reduced the production of charcoal, and so of iron. One can, however, safely say that the work done in the "Fifties" and "Sixties" of last century definitely removed all anxiety with regard to the supply of steel. The question of *quality* was, and is, however, a very different matter. In 1920 I heard the late Sir J. Roper Wright tell the President of the Iron and Steel Institute—that eminent metallurgist, the late Dr. Stead—that in 1865, working with the first small Siemens furnace in Birmingham, he had endeavoured to eliminate phosphorus and sulphur from steel, and that metallurgists were still working on the same problem. These impurities, which at times we engineers are in dread of, are capable of reduction to safe proportions, but in many cases at a cost we do not wish to pay. The first great step was taken in 1876, when S. G. Thomas announced the possibility of the reduction of phosphorus by using a furnace lining of basic material, which he and his cousin, Gilchrist, had discovered. The announcement was made at the March meeting of the Iron and Steel Institute, and one of our old members, the late Mr. Henry Webb of Bury, who showed at some of our meetings that kindly interest in me when a young man which one never forgets, described the incident to me very vividly. Mr. Thomas spoke with hesitation and nervousness at the end of the meeting, when many members had left, and though little attention was paid to what he said at the time, the announcement was really of the greatest importance, not only to engineers, but to the world at large, opening as it did so large a field of supplies of steel for engineering purposes.

The supply of materials was assured by the processes I have mentioned, and these were devised in a comparatively short time. But the improvements in those materials which have meant so much to us in providing lighter structures with increased safety, more durable metal, and the capacity for carrying out more work with greater satisfaction and in less time, have been of somewhat slow growth, and naturally have not reached finality yet. There are three of these improvements that I would like to touch upon, namely the effect of heat-treatment on metals; the knowledge of their microstructure; and the introduction of steel and other alloys, which have provided and are still providing better materials. In the first two cases we have further instances of the interdependence of the sciences, for it has been the development of physics that has led to the progress that has been achieved.

The heat-treatment of steel undoubtedly started when by accident some primitive steel worker found that the quenching of the hot mass he had produced gave it a hardness that was probably at first a problem and a trouble to him, but afterwards of the greatest value to engineers. The effects of simple treatment were known to our first President, but it was not until the pyrometer came into more general use that we were able, by its aid, together with that of micrography and macrography, to get absolutely reliable information with regard to the steels produced. One should, however, never forget the pioneer work done by scientists, which has led to what is now our everyday practice in the treatment of metals. It would be impossible to name all of those to whom engineers are indebted, but one cannot pass on without mentioning Sorby, Osmond, Roberts-Austen, and Le Chatelier, amongst the number who come to mind. I have already said that it may be thought that I am giving a too special prominence to metallurgy, but the very platform from which I am speaking is the most historical spot in existence in connexion with the co-operation of engineering and metallurgy.

There have been few committees formed by an Institution like our own, which have been so successful in their work, not only for the members of the Institution which formed them but for the world at large, as the Alloys Research Committee formed by this Institution in October 1889, I believe at the suggestion of Dr. William Anderson. Our President was then Mr. Charles Cochrane, and the committee consisted of Dr. (late Sir) William Anderson (Chairman), Sir Frederick Abel, Professor (later Sir) W. C. Roberts-Austen, Mr. (later Sir) Edward H. Carbutt, Professor D. E. Hughes, Professor (later Sir) Alexander B. W. Kennedy, Mr. Arthur Paget, Mr. Joseph Tomlinson, and Professor W. Cawthorne Unwin. In all eleven reports, spread over thirty years, were made, and the authors included such eminent men as Roberts-Austen, Gowland, Carpenter, Hadfield, Longmuir, Edwards, and finally Rosenhain and his assistants.

The Committee desired that the first metal to be dealt with should be iron, but very wisely Professor Roberts-Austen deferred this work until certain elementary matters dealing with alloys generally should have been investigated. I count myself extremely fortunate in having been able to be present at meetings in this hall when some of the earlier reports were presented, and when the discussions between Professor Roberts-Austen and Professor Arnold did so much to clear up our difficulties with regard to the state in which iron itself exists in the materials we use. When the Sixth Report was read in January 1904, the President, Mr. J. Hartley Wicksteed, quoted at the conclusion of the discussion the words of Sir William Roberts-Austen, and said, " In the future it will be realized how much The Institution of Mechanical Engineers has done to confirm, strengthen and diffuse the knowledge we possess on the important industrial question of hardening steel." *

The questions of heat-treatment and micrography were dealt with very fully in those reports, and undoubtedly they are classical documents on these matters. I shall speak later of the reports on non-ferrous metals. It is perhaps well to remember that we are still carrying on the work initiated by our Institution nearly forty years ago, and are associated with the Alloys of Iron Research Committee which is working under the Chairmanship of our Past-President, Sir John Dewrance, who has shown such generous interest in all research of this character. If I might refer members to a meeting of our Graduates and an actual example of heat-treatment, I would mention the table with microphotographs of tyre steel which I showed at the Graduates' Meeting on 27th February 1922. In this a piece of tyre steel was shown as having in one case a tenacity of 40·6 tons per sq. in., with 34·0 per cent elongation, and in another case raised to 79·8 tons per sq. in. with 14·5 per cent elongation.

The subject of metallography is so closely associated with the heat-treatment which the metals receive that it is very difficult to separate them. It is, of course, owing to the possibility of examining the structure of metals under the microscope that we have been able to follow so closely the effect of heat-treatment upon them. Here we have to thank Dr. Sorby, the geologist, who in 1863 turned from the examination of geological specimens to an investigation of the structure of metals. In 1886 and 1887 he read his Papers on "The Microscopical Structure of Iron and Steel," † in which he showed the true structure of pearlite, and since that date the study and examination of metals through the microscope has become an everyday part of the work of the metallurgist. As the work of Whitworth has given us means of close and accurate measurement, so the work of Sorby of Sheffield has given us means of determining closely and accurately the heat-treatment any particular steel has received.

Work is still progressing in this direction. Some time ago Dr. Rosenhain worked on the use of ultra-violet rays in connexion with metallography with high magnifications. Recently I have seen ‡ some very remarkable microphotographs of steel taken in this

---

* Proc. I. Mech. E., 1904, vol. i. page 91.
† Journal of the Iron and Steel Institute, 1886, part 1, page 140; 1887, part 1, page 255.
‡ International Testing Congress, Amsterdam, September 1927, F. F. Lucas, Bell Telephone Research Laboratory. "A résumé of the development and application of high-power metallography and the ultra-violet microscope."

way at a magnification of 3,500 on to the lantern plate. The picture on the screen represented an area of steel having a diameter of under 0·0017 inch; or about one six-hundreth of an inch.

This leads me to point out that much as micrography has helped us, we should never forget the very limited field to which it is, of necessity, confined, even with fairly low magnifications. Dr. Carpenter has pointed this out in his introduction to a recent book,* and states very truly that macrography should precede micrography. This is a most important point for all engineers and in many cases the taking of a sulphur print, which for a large section can be obtained in a few minutes, will give interesting information. It is a process I personally use very frequently. The limitation of the field of investigation by the use of a tensile test-bar 0·564 inch in diameter as against one 0·798 inch in diameter is also a matter about which I am seriously concerned, as it halves our opportunity of observing non-metallic enclosures or other imperfections.

There is one point in the work of the Alloys Research Committee which might well be remembered. In the Fifth Report in 1899, Sir William C. Roberts-Austen said that the Research Committee of The Institution of Mechanical Engineers had exerted a noteworthy influence in connexion with the preliminary inquiry, the result of which led to the recommendation that a National Physical Laboratory should be established. It is not necessary for me to emphasize what this great Institution has done and is doing for us as engineers. We have only to imagine what our position would have been to-day if it had not been founded.

The question of alloy, or special steels, is a very large one, and I can only touch briefly on it and its important bearing on mechanical engineering. In reality, all steel comes under the category of alloy steel, but general usage confines the term to steels containing a specially added substance other than carbon.

As far back as 1821, Faraday published a work on "Alloys of Steel," and experimented with alloys both of nickel and chrome, but neither he nor Berthier, who worked shortly afterwards in France on similar lines, carried the work into the industrial world. The same may generally be said of a group of experimenters who worked both in Europe and America in the late "Sixties" and early "Seventies" of last century. One exception is the work of the Mushets, who about 1857 brought out their self-hardening tool steel,

---

* Introduction to "Metallography and Macrography," by Guillet and Portevin.

with tungsten as the essential alloying metal. Even this was not followed up, although its comparatively excellent practical qualities always remain vividly impressed on my memory when I think of the steps I took forty years ago, as an apprentice at a lathe, to possess—and keep—tools of this make of steel. It was not until many years afterwards that the work of White in America, about 1900, showed that by increasing the amount of tungsten and chromium, steel would not soften at high temperatures, and thus cutting speeds could be multiplied many times. It is a well-known fact that this led to almost wholesale scrapping of machines, as no longer was the tool the weak link in the production chain, but the design of the machine itself. Various improvements in tool steel have taken place since that time, especially with a view to ascertaining the best alloys for special purposes.

The greatest distinct advance in alloys of iron took place in 1882, when Mr. (now Sir) Robert A. Hadfield started his experimental work with an investigation of steel and manganese, the early results of which were first published in the Papers he read before the Institution of Civil Engineers in 1888.* This material possesses extraordinary qualities of resistance to wear, which make it indispensable for some of our work. This historic Paper was very shortly followed † by a Paper on iron and silicon, an alloy which has revolutionized the construction of transformers and other electrical apparatus owing to its low hysteresis value. Sir Robert Hadfield honoured us by reading a Paper on the alloys of iron and molybdenum before our Institution in 1915.‡ The earlier Papers referred to marked another of the great metallurgical advances in connexion with mechanical engineering, for they dealt with industrial as well as scientific questions. The investigations of Sir Robert A. Hadfield included also alloys of iron with aluminium, chromium, nickel, tungsten, etc. These are classical works, and are also valuable on account of the complete manner in which they deal with comparatively simple alloys, and not only placed metallurgists and engineers under the greatest obligation to Sir Robert A. Hadfield, but have placed this country in an enviable position in regard to pioneer work in this direction.

It has often been said, and with every truth, that the alloys of steel, notably those with chromium and nickel, have made possible the mechanical revolution which has taken place through the

---

* Proc. Inst. C. E., vol. xciii, pages 1 and 61.
† Journal, Iron and Steel Institute, 1889, part 2, page 222.
‡ Proc. I. Mech. E., 1915, page 701.

autocar and the aeroplane. There is now no difficulty in obtaining steels with a tenacity of over 100 tons per sq. in. with an elongation of 9 per cent on 2 inches. Our only difficulty is to decide when it is advantageous to use these from a commercial standpoint. Advance has also been made in higher carbon steels with high yield-points for shipbuilding and other purposes. Undoubtedly we shall before long be considering the use of such steels, or else of nickel and other alloy steels, for boilers, since we have pressures up to 3,200 lb. per sq. in. in use for stationary boilers, and up to 1,400 lb. per sq. in. in locomotive practice. In the latter case a 3 per cent nickel-steel is actually being used.

The use of high pressures is a matter of great importance, for we have also to deal with a " new " phenomenon in the physical condition of steel at the temperatures that we are likely to have to use. As in many other cases, so in the case of the " creep " of steel at high temperatures, we find that it has been known and worked on for many years, but it is only now being investigated with the knowledge of its practical importance. In the last few years Papers of great value have been read by J. H. S. Dickenson,* and before our Institution in 1924 by Dr. F. C. Lea.† An appreciation of the practical value of these investigations is shown by the reference to the subject by our Past-President, Mr. William H. Patchell, in his Presidential Address in 1924, and by the Paper read before the Institution by Professor A. L. Mellanby and Dr. William Kerr last session.‡ Dr. Kerr also read a Paper on " Failure of Metals by Creep " at Glasgow in 1926. § This year we have had two reassuring Papers on the subject. In April Mr. R. W. Bailey read a Paper before the North Western Branch of our Institution and was led to the conclusion that " creep " always exists but that at ordinary temperatures the rate is too small to be detected. At the Autumn Meeting of the Iron and Steel Institute Dr. W. Rosenhain and Dr. D. Hanson gave the results of their experiments in stressing mild steel for between five and six years at a temperature of 300° C. and showed that little change took place. Although the subject is difficult, it is therefore probably one upon which we can look from an engineering standpoint without misgiving.

There has been in the last few years a great advance in the use of chromium as an alloy of steel, although, as I have mentioned,

---

* Journal, Iron and Steel Institute, 1922, vol. cvi, page 103.
† Proc. I. Mech. E., 1924, vol. ii, page 1,053.
‡ Proc. I. Mech. E., 1927, vol. i, page 53.
§ Trans. Inst. Engrs. and Shipbdrs. in Scotland, 1925-26, vol. 69, page 319.

Faraday and Berthier experimented in this direction over 100 years ago. We naturally appreciate the non-oxidizing advantages of this material, but the price prevents its general commercial employment, notwithstanding the fact that its uses for special purposes are growing rapidly. Its capability of resisting high temperatures has made it indispensable for valves in many internal-combustion engines.

Before I pass on from this part of my subject, I would like to mention a minor use of alloy steel for that early mechanical engineering tool, the chisel. In 1916 the Institution did me the honour of allowing me to read a small contribution on this subject,* in which I dealt with straight carbon steel. During the discussion, Sir Robert Hadfield suggested that a trial might be made with alloy steels. The War prevented these experiments being at once carried out, but at its conclusion the matter was put in hand. On the advice of Sir Robert Hadfield, the steels selected for research were :—

1. Nickel-Chrome Steel.
2. Nickel Steel.
3. Chrome-Vanadium Steel.

After consideration, it was decided that the steel ought to possess the following properties :—

(1) The composition should be such that it would be flexible enough to meet various requirements and thus render a combination of different steels unnecessary.
(2) That it should harden or toughen at one heating and require no tempering—in other words, that it should be a non-tempering steel.

Many compositions of these steels were used in this research, and the results plainly indicated that the first two were about equal and more suitable than the chrome-vanadium steel. It was finally proved that a simple nickel-steel of the following composition would best meet the conditions laid down :—

Combined Carbon	0·38–0·42 per cent
Nickel	3·00–3·50 ,,
Manganese (max.)	0·60 ,,

Further, it was found that any departure from these limits seriously interfered with the combination of properties. Thus, if the proportion of carbon were about 0·5 per cent, the tendency was to harden, and tempering became necessary, while if it fell below 0·38 per cent, the steel became too soft ; hence the fixing of the

---

* Proc. I. Mech. E., 1916, page 141.

above specification. Similar remarks apply to the nickel content. The conditions of treatment are as follows :—

> After forging, heat to 900°–925° C.
> Quench in linseed oil (raw).
> No further treatment required.

The cutting edge should be prepared with a file. This steel has now been in use in the Derby locomotive shops for the last two years, and has given every satisfaction. The following figures show how it compares with carbon steel :—

> Carbon-steel chisels issued per week in fitting shop for 1921–22–23. Average 127, or 6,350 per year of 50 weeks, or 18 per man per year (350 fitters).
> Nickel-steel in same shop (all carbon-steel chisels having been removed or called in). After equipping the shop, during the first year, 434 chisels were issued to replace those coming in for repair. This equals 6·7 per week, or 1·2 per man per year.

The cost of the chisels at present prices is about the same, whether made of plain carbon steel or of nickel-steel.

Since the problem of chisels has been dealt with, the same steel has been successfully used for all classes of smiths' and boilermakers' sets and hand snaps, and for many other tools. This steel is the only one now used for these classes of tool. It has also been found that modified treatment renders it suitable for such purposes as pneumatic riveting tools, and this use of the material is now receiving attention. At the time the composition and treatment were being investigated, the manufacture of the steel was also considered. It was found that hammered bars were much better than rolled material, particularly with regard to freedom from " roaks " and other surface defects, and this condition is now a part of the specification.

A consideration of non-ferrous metals at once shows that an ever-increasing range of metals and their alloys has become available for our use. At the period I have taken as a basis, the work of Muntz was already known, but it was much later before full advantage was taken of the properties of the brass which goes by his name. When articles were produced in small quantities the property of a brass which enabled it to be easily hot-worked had not the same commercial advantage as when production became greater. Now the most intricate forms of stampings and complicated extruded sections are available when we wish to use them for mass production. The use of non-ferrous alloys of this and similar types was for long retarded because in the majority of cases, although practically non-corrosive, their strength was less than that of ferrous materials. The advance which has been made in this direction, however, can be best shown by quoting the British Engineering Standards Association Specification No. 208–1924 for High Tensile Brass Castings which calls for a tensile strength of 45 tons per sq. in. with 12 per cent elongation, and for High Tensile Brass Bars which requires 28 tons per sq. in. with 25 per cent elongation on a gauge length not less than four times the diameter. Even higher figures of tensile strength or elongation are available and a whole range of different alloys comes in this class which includes the so-called "manganese-bronze." Progress here, if slow, has finally been great.

Aluminium was not known commercially until about thirty-five years ago, and even in 1913 the world's production was only 64,000 tons. In 1926, however, this had risen to 235,000 tons, or 3·67 times as much. Although in its pure state it is not generally satisfactory for our work, when alloyed with small proportions of other metals it is becoming invaluable. The Ninth, Tenth and Eleventh Reports of our Alloys Research Committee did much to show what wonderful properties can be obtained from these alloys to meet various requirements. The work of the Light Alloy Sub-Committee of the Aeronautical Advisory Committee, in conjunction with these reports, shows what a wide range of requirements can be covered. One should perhaps specially refer to the monumental Eleventh Report of our Alloys Research Committee which is one of the most complete and exhaustive research reports ever published. The qualities of the "Y" alloy which Dr. Rosenhain described there, and of duralumin, have placed entirely new materials at our disposal. The "Y" alloy gives in the hot-rolled condition a tensile stress of 17·6 tons per sq. in., with an elongation of 20·0 per cent on 2 inches, and when quenched a stress of 24·1 tons per sq. in. with an elongation of 23·0 per cent. Owing to its lightness this material is specially suitable for reciprocating parts and for aeronautical purposes. The specific gravity of duralumin is only 2·8 as compared with 7·8 for steel, and in sheet form the tensile stress ranges from 25 to 35 tons per sq. in. with an elongation of 20 to 25 per cent according to whether it is in the normal or hard condition. In rod form duralumin will give a stress of 26 tons per sq. in. with 18 per cent elongation (normal) and a stress of 32 tons per sq. in. with 6 to 10 per cent elongation (hard). It seems somewhat surprising that the chief use of these new materials is so far practically confined to aeronautical purposes, and for certain parts of motor-car work, although they have been known for so long, and in the case of the smaller internal-combustion high-speed engine have become universally employed for pistons. They can be used either as castings or forgings.

In addition to the essentially light alloys, aluminium bronzes can also be employed either as castings or forgings, and gear-wheels of this material have found an extensive application. The recent development of centrifugally cast phosphor-bronze gears should also be noted.

There are certain purposes in our work for which a metal which will resist oxidization at high temperatures is advantageous. In the last few years much investigation has taken place in this direction. We now have certain alloys of chromium and nickel which are fairly easily cast and have this property to a marked degree. They are extremely useful for case-hardening pots and other articles subjected to an oxidizing flame. Their only disadvantage is that at present their first cost seems high, and for articles which have to be replaced the dictum of a friend (the head of a large industrial research laboratory) that "quality is remembered long after cost has been forgotten" does not always hold good. In addition to their use in castings these two metals in various percentages and combined in the former with copper and in the latter with chromium and iron can be rolled and forged and should come into increasing use. One should also mention the "natural" alloy of copper and nickel called after the late Col. Monel. This was one of the first of this type of non-ferrous alloys put to practical use.

Nickel by itself, in which Canada is so particularly interested, has not many uses at present. It is, however, not only being used for plating, but to an increasing extent for deposition. New knowledge has enabled us to produce deposits of very great hardness which allow of the successful building up of worn parts, and this is especially useful in the smaller internal-combustion engines used in automobile and aeronautical work.

There are also certain metals which we have been in the habit of looking upon as rare, or semi-rare, which are now coming into use for our work. Of these perhaps the most important is magnesium, which gives us an additional base for another series of most interesting light alloys. At present it is practically unknown in this country. During the War experiments were made with this metal as a constituent of what may be called aluminium light alloys, but these did not give the results hoped for. It is, however, only of recent years that the manufacture of this metal has taken place on such a scale as to allow it to be produced at a commercial price. In Germany great progress has been made in the last few years in alloys in which the proportion of magnesium is in the neighbourhood of 90 per cent. It may be pointed out that whilst the specific gravity of aluminium is 2·67, that of magnesium is only 1·74, and therefore we have at our service a metal which is even lighter than what we have been accustomed to look upon as our lightest material, and which I am afraid has been regarded in the past for this very reason with unwarranted suspicion. I think that aluminium has for long suffered from this and from having been pushed forward in early days as a pure metal for purposes for which it was not suitable. The knowledge we now have should prevent magnesium from being prejudiced in this way. In Germany, where the production and use of magnesium alloys has been developed, they are being largely used in place of aluminium alloys for pistons and other parts of motor-cars. They have the advantages of being extremely easy to machine, they can be readily forged and extruded, and recent developments have provided alloys of greatly improved strength compared with any magnesium alloys hitherto available, both in the cast and worked conditions.

Cadmium has a great advantage as a metal to be used for plating, for it possesses high corrosion-resisting properties. It is also valuable for use as an alloy of copper in telephone wires, and for overhead conductors for tramways, where it adds considerably to the resistance to wear and has also good electrical conductivity. Cadmium is also coming into use for solders, and as a constituent of bearing metals. Its availability for industrial application is clearly indicated by its price, which at present is considerably lower than that of tin.

I have already referred to the advantage of chromium in alloy with iron and nickel. When used for plating it also gives greater resistance to an oxidizing flame, and is finding applications in industrial plant quite beyond the ordinary plating field.

Cobalt, tungsten, vanadium, and molybdenum are chiefly used as alloys of steel, but it may be that before long they will be available for special uses in a basic form, and, in fact, tungsten is used in electric lamps at the present time.

The science of measurement or metrology may seem to be part of our ordinary work, and the greatest step forward ever made was when Whitworth (to use the words of his Presidential Address in

1856 *) first considered "the vast importance of attending to the two great elements in constructive mechanics, namely, a *true plane* and the *power of measurement.* "The latter," he said, "cannot be attained without the former, which is, therefore, of primary importance. All excellence of workmanship depends on it." It is pleasing to think that two of the actual surface planes used by Whitworth are the property of the Whitworth Society, who have entrusted us with their custody. This matter of accurate measurement, on which all interchangeability depends, received a great impetus during the War, and through the work of Sir Richard Glazebrook and his colleagues at the National Physical Laboratory it was placed on a far better commercial basis. It would be as impertinent as it is unnecessary for me to endeavour to add to the words of the Address of our Past-President which I have quoted.

In physics we are all intensely interested in the general structure of matter, on which so much research has been done in recent years, and about which we have still so much to learn. We are fortunate in having this year for our Thomas Hawksley lecturer one who has done such brilliant work in this direction as Sir William H. Bragg, and we look forward to what he will have to tell us of his work. I am not aiming at prophecy when I say that I, like many others, believe we are on the threshold of some solution of the all-important problem of cohesion. In 1923, at the Liverpool Meeting of the British Association, the Engineering Section joined with the Physical and Mathematical Sections in a discussion on "Cohesion." An incident in the discussion will make clear its importance to us. Sir Oliver Lodge, referring to a remark I had made, said he supposed my desire was to know why, when he lifted one end of his stick up, the other end followed, whereas Dr. F. C. Lea pointed out that our trouble as engineers was not so much this as to know why, when the stick had been lifted say a hundred million times, it broke when an effort was made to lift it the hundred million and first time. Knowledge which would assure us of greater cohesion of matter as we use it, or of warning when it was going to cease to cohere, would in many cases be invaluable to us.

A large number of Papers of the greatest value have been written on "fatigue," and there are many different methods of applying repetition stresses to material. We are learning slowly why we cannot stress our materials to a higher limit than we do to-day without such material finally ceasing to cohere, and we look to our physicists to enlighten us more on this point, and to allow us to

---

* Proc. I. Mech. E., 1856, page 127.

assure ourselves of that perfect safety which is the first essential of all our work.

Physics is also helping us, and is likely to do so more as advances are made in the science of radiology. What we cannot see, but know may exist, is frequently a trouble and anxiety to us who deal with metals, whether cast or forged. The advance made in recent years has been most marked, and whereas in 1918 the greatest thickness of steel which could be penetrated by radiography was 1 inch, $4\frac{1}{2}$ inches can now be dealt with. Already radiography is being extensively used for the inspection of welds and castings, and of completely assembled small parts, as is done at Woolwich, and of glued wood, etc. It brings to our notice again the question of the commercial application of the facilities at our disposal. Messrs. Pullin and Wiltshire, in their recent book * very truly say : " The radiologist does not know the problems of industry. He can only offer his rays as a new tool to the industrialist, and leave it to him to suggest the particular problems in his own sphere which they may help to serve."

I think that one of the most remarkable Papers read before the Institution in recent years on the lines of which I am speaking was that presented in 1917 by A. A. Griffith and G. I. Taylor. This was entitled " The Use of Soap Films in Solving Torsion Problems." † In the position I then occupied I had to deal with the administration side of the work on which this Paper was based, and I frankly admit that as an ordinary, so-called practical engineer it was some time before I appreciated the simplicity and accuracy of the apparatus and the far-reaching result achieved by it. It has allowed us to determine without great expense the torsional stresses set up in complicated sections which could not be dealt with on mathematical lines. I only wish we could determine in as simple a way the stresses in the various parts of the complicated section of a locomotive tyre when shrunk on to a wheel centre.

Those very beautiful experiments that have led to our being able to determine the nature of the stresses on cutting tools, etc., by optical means, which have been developed by Professor Coker, are well known to all our members. On a somewhat similar principle there has recently been placed on the market for commercial use an instrument for examining glass and other transparent substances. This allows one to ascertain the inherent internal stresses in articles made of such materials, and is being applied to the examination of

---

* " X-Rays, Past and Present " (Benn), 1927.
† Proc. I. Mech. E., 1917, page 755.

gauge-glasses amongst other things. One could wish that we were far enough advanced to deal with metals in a similarly easy way.

In attempting such a review as this one becomes more and more convinced of the interdependence I have previously spoken of, and it is practically impossible to separate the work of various branches of science. This is perhaps nowhere more marked than in the case of chemistry. It is due to the advance in the accuracy of this science that we are able to determine the effect of minute quantities of various elements in our material. With what small proportions chemists deal is perhaps not so often recognized as it would be if instead of saying 0·001 per cent we said one hundred-thousandth part. I do not mean to suggest that actual analyses are accurate to within such narrow limits, but I know that we expect results of analyses to agree within three one hundred-thousandth parts when dealing with the determination of such important impurities as sulphur and phosphorus in steel.

One of the greatest facilities we have received in our practical work of recent years has been the development of means of easily cutting and welding the metals we deal with. This is now very readily done by the aid of intense local heat generated in various ways. The first, and probably still the most generally used, is by means of the oxy-acetylene flame. Our ability to use this is the result of steady progressive work by chemists culminating in the production of calcium carbide in the electric furnace by Moissan in 1894. It was accidentally produced independently at the same time by T. L. Willson. Recent uses to which the flame has been put include the hardening of gear-wheel teeth under water.

The chemists' investigations in connexion with crude oils both from petroleum and shale have resulted in the comprehensive range of liquid fuels and lubricating oils which are available at the present day, and such fuels from natural sources have been supplemented by others which are synthetically prepared.

Certain oils with other constituents give us protective paints, and it is often a lack of chemical knowledge or information which causes us to employ paints which are not absolutely suitable for the purpose and conditions under which they are used.

The matter of lubrication is one in which we have to work in close co-operation with the chemist and physicist. Largely due to lack of this co-operation many failures have occurred in the past. It is not always possible for us to design our mechanism so that we can lubricate bearings in the best possible manner, but we should always have this in mind. We require also to have the knowledge, which is generally available, of the most suitable class of lubricant, and at what viscosity it is best for our purpose. Much discussion and research has taken place as to the means to be adopted to give true and economical lubrication without the risk of failure of the mechanism owing to metals being allowed to come in contact. The knowledge gained and the progress made has been considerable, and as a result we are now rarely seriously troubled in this respect, and we trust that the work which is still going on may lead to even better results and still greater economy. This, however, will only be achieved by the co-operation which here and elsewhere is so essential, and by the realization that the chemist does not always see matters in the light which has come to us from years of work and, I trust, observation.

There are many other sciences which help us to achieve the objects of our profession in a more satisfactory way that I can do little more than mention. For instance, I have not and cannot deal with the benefits we have derived from the advances of mathematical knowledge in so many directions. The study of the effects of environment and the causes of fatigue have received much attention of recent years, whilst the analysis of the causation of accidents is likely to give us useful results.

Closer attention to the methods employed in education, both technical and practical, is being given with a view of utilizing to better advantage the time which is thus spent. Here, too, the Institution has recently played a great part. Thanks so largely to the work done and the interest shown by Dr. Hele-Shaw, we have, as all our members know, instituted in co-operation with the Board of Education the National Certificates and Diplomas, and so standardized at a high level much of the engineering education of this country. It is pleasing to notice that this is being followed in other branches of technical work.

It is with some hesitation that one speaks of another subject that is ever present with practically all of us. The subject of industrial psychology has received much and increasing attention in recent years. Some of our Universities have Chairs in the general subject, and much research work is being done. One can only trust that close touch will be kept with practical work in this direction, work which, although we may not always recognize it, we are doing every day in the ordinary course of our duties. There is no doubt that there is an improved feeling between men generally, if at times the rate of progress may seem to fluctuate, and one can only trust that the progress may be steady and at an increasing rate. One of our great novelists has, I believe, prophesied that the next great advance in civilization will be in the direction of this science.

As we have always, if unconsciously, been psychologists, so too we have been economists, and here also increasing attention is being given to methods by which we may accurately and readily ascertain our position in this respect.

It may be thought that I am wandering from the subject with which I set out to deal, but it is only because of the length of my Address that I do not deal more fully with these and other most important questions which are ever before us. In this somewhat hasty and admittedly incomplete review of the assistance we have received as mechanical engineers from work not directly connected with our own, I may seem to have given not only the first but by far the greatest attention to metallurgy. This is to a large extent inevitable, for it is through the existence of the metals that we have ceased to be "hewers of wood and drawers of water." We have advanced as the materials at our disposal have advanced. Great as has been the assistance which we have received from the related sciences, and great as is the indebtedness of metallurgy to them, the advantages we derive are dependent upon our being able to find at hand the material we require in order to adopt the developments made possible by those sciences.

At the present time we are witnessing one of the greatest practical steps forward ever made, namely, that involving the use of much higher pressures and the employment of greatly increased temperatures. The materials in general use a few years ago are, or soon will be, unsuitable for our growing requirements. But this need not cause us any real anxiety, for there will undoubtedly be materials ready for our needs.

Sometimes one is apt to forget the large number of brilliant men who in various positions are working on problems whose solution will allow manufacturers of materials to get ahead of our requirements. One sign of the times is the employment on research by practically all our steel and metal makers of metallurgists and metallurgical chemists. I know of no body of men who are more earnestly endeavouring to co-ordinate industry and science, and I would appeal to you to assist them in every possible way by discussing not only your difficulties but your successes with them.

The progress we have made and are still making has been due to research, even if it has not always been recognized by that name. The work done by individual firms is not only helpful but absolutely necessary, for one can then freely deal with the products of the firm in the conditions under which they are employed. There is, however, the wider question of general research, and if we are to make the greatest possible progress in the future it is necessary that this should continue on a still larger scale. Several of our larger firms have research departments. In the National Physical Laboratory, in whose inception, as I have mentioned, we were concerned, and in conjunction with which we are working in the Alloys of Iron Research, we have probably the finest general research institution in the world. Many of our University laboratories are engaged on special work, and the results of some of this have formed the subjects of recent Papers read before us, notably Dr. F. C. Lea's Papers on "The Effect of Temperature on Materials." * Yet in spite of this one feels that research receives far greater attention in America and Germany. The Bell Testing Laboratory in New York, for instance, is a large building of ten floors covering a block and employing 4,000 investigators and assistants.†

But valuable as researches are when conducted on these lines, I feel that research of the kind that is conducted jointly by scientists and practical men should receive more attention than it does at present. It is under such conditions that a wide view may be taken, and that the whole issue can be dealt with on the broadest possible basis. I would like to call attention to the work done by the British Non-ferrous Metals Research Association, and by the more recently formed British Cast Iron Research Association. These bodies, largely composed of and supported by manufacturers of the metals they deal with, and by engineers who use such products, are doing valuable work, but their activities are not so great as they deserve to be, owing to their not receiving the full support of the industry.

I have endeavoured to show that the progress we have made during the past eighty years is largely due to work not directly connected with our own daily duties. Research will undoubtedly give us information which will allow our progress to continue, if not always as quickly as we would desire. It is, therefore, incumbent upon us to take advantage of the assistance at hand as quickly as possible. In the past this has not always been done. This may be due to the necessity of considering immediate commercial results, which may sometimes make us impatient with research. We make the mistake of expecting results similar to those from our machines, forgetting that mechanical production follows well-known laws long

---

* Proc. I. Mech. E., 1922, page 885; 1924, page 1,053.
† International Congress for Testing Materials, Amsterdam, September 1927 (Mr. F. F. Lucas).

tried out. The research worker is the pioneer, often working in practically unknown lands and with little to guide him, and I think he must himself frequently be discouraged by not making the progress he desires. He is the explorer finding the path along which we may progress.

It has been said that the training of an engineer is one which tends to dull or blunt the imagination. This may or may not be true, but the assistance we receive from those not directly connected with engineering will always be great. It lies with us to use to the fullest extent the tools they forge for us and the knowledge they place at our disposal. Their work must always differ from ours, and, appreciating this, we must for our own sakes give what assistance we can. We are chiefly concerned with design, production, and output, and once having settled our course of action we push forward on a definite path. The research worker must constantly be considering the next step he is to take. A fairly close description of the searcher occurred to one who, writing over 2,000 years ago, said :—

> "This wisdom of the scribe cometh by the opportunity of leisure ; and he that hath little business shall become wise." *

Whilst of those of us who are endeavouring to apply that wisdom he said :—

> "They will maintain the fabric of the world ; and in the handywork of their craft is their prayer." †

Vote of Thanks.

Sir JOHN A. F. ASPINALL, D.Eng. (*Past-President*), proposed a vote of thanks to the President for his Address. Sir Henry had come to him as a young engineer to learn the rudiments of his work, and he was proud to see that he had now become President of the Institution. During the eighty years since George Stephenson had occupied the Presidential Chair, there had been forty-two Presidents, of whom he had known personally thirty-three. Seven of the forty-two Past-Presidents had been locomotive engineers and had naturally given to the Institution an account of their locomotive work. Sir Henry, however, had largely dealt with metallurgical matters; he was not surprised at this for Sir Henry had taken a keen interest in metallurgy from the earliest days he had known him. About forty years ago the title of an engineer in charge of railway rolling stock had been changed from Locomotive Superintendent to Chief Mechanical Engineer, because his duties had become wider and necessitated a knowledge of metallurgy, chemistry, physics and kindred subjects. As Chief Mechanical Engineer of the London, Midland and Scottish Railway, Sir Henry had charge of works at Crewe, Derby, Horwich, St. Rollox and other places, each equipped with a good chemical laboratory and adequate testing appliances, and so it was possible for him to add to his already wide experience. There were opportunities of research which enabled him or his assistants to present Papers upon engineering subjects which had been of great interest. As indicating the magnitude of mechanical engineering on the railways, it was perhaps not generally realized that there were about 120,000 skilled mechanics engaged upon the construction and maintenance of rolling stock, and the rarity of accidents due to mechanical defects testified to the care which the Chief Mechanical Engineers of the four great railways of this country bestowed upon the study of materials.

Dr. H. S. HELE-SHAW, F.R.S. (*Past-President*), seconded the vote of thanks to the President and said that to do so was an honour which he valued because he had known him for most of the thirty years during which Sir Henry had been connected with the Institution. He had also known him as a young man when he had gained a Whitworth Exhibition. He supported Sir John Aspinall's remarks as to the President's ability and experience, which well fitted him to deliver from personal knowledge so comprehensive an Address; he earnestly commended the Address to every member for further study. He added that they were proud of the services that Sir Henry had rendered his country during the War and to the cause of education, and of the honours which had been conferred upon him.

Acknowledgements

I am indebted to the following people and organisations for their help and guidance in the research and compilation of this book:

Alan Butcher (Ian Allan Publishing), Richard Casserley, David Cross, Stan Brotherton, Dennis Cameron, and Pam Stevens (Spondon Historical Society), The Archivists of Birmingham and Manchester Universities, The Middleton Press, Professor Robert Davies (Professor of Mechanical Engineering the University of Birmingham), David Snowden, Bernard Roberts (Prince Henry's High School), *The Railway Magazine*, The Institution of Mechanical Engineers, Gerald Heath, The 'Kings Own' Royal Regiment Museum, the Staff of Evesham Library, the staff at the Almonry, and Mary my wife.

Photo 33: Port Street in flood c 1890. Fowlers Shop Nos. 8 & 9 (white shop front), is on right at the edge of flood line. This was Sir Henry's birthplace. Deacle's School railings can be seen just below the shop.

Photo 34: Fowler's Shop in High Street c 1930

Index

A

Aberdeen 77
Acetylene Gas for Lighting *12*
Aden 78
Advisory Committee for Aeronautics 37
Aircraft Mission 37
America 14, 48, 71
American Captain 39
Anderson, James 14
Aspinall, John 10, 12
Assistant to the Vice President of Scientific Research 73
Association of Locomotive Engineers 18
Association of Railway Engineers 24, 46
Austin 34
Australia 78

B

Badsey 8
Barlett 53
Bayliss, Alf 52
Beames, H.P.M. 48
Belpaire 27
Bengeworth 3, 4, 51, 52, 54, 85
Bengeworth Station 85
Beyer-Garratt 60
Beyer-Peacock 60
Bible Class 13, 20, 25, 32, 38, 43, 44, 60, 78
Big Bertha 42
Bird, Charlie 52

Birmingham 62, 63, 64, 85
Birmingham Art School 7
Birth **5**
Bishop of Sydney 78
Board of Directors 17, 29
Board of Education 64
Board of Management 18, 26
Boer War 32
Bombay 78
Bomber Command 79, 82
Bretforton 4
Bristol 85, 86
Britain 12, 32, 35, 41, 47
Britannia Class Pacific 59
British Association 50, 54, 77, 89
British Rail 24
Bromsgrove 22, 30
Brunel 3, 10
Buckingham Palace 35

C

Cairo 74, 75, 89
Cambridge 77
Canada 37, 54, 68
Canadian Pacific 54
Captain of the Bell Ringers 43
Carlisle 57, 58
Chelleston, Derby 14
Chief Mechanical Engineer 10, 11, 17, 18, 20, 23, 26, 41, 43, 47
Chief Motive Power Superintendent 20, 23
Chorley 10
Church Assembly 65
Church of England 4
Churchward, G.J. 22, 26

Civil Engineering 22
Civil Engineers 11, 12, 89
Clare College, Cambridge 76
Classification of Power 27
College of Arms 37
Collett, C. 26
Colombo 78
Committee of Noise Prevention 79
Conference on Standardisation of Aircraft Components 37
Crewe 48, 49, 56, 77

D

Darley Dale 43
Deeley 13, 16, 17, 22, 27, 56, 59
Deputy Director-General of Aircraft Production 37
Derby 12, 13, 14, 19, 21, 24, 25, 28, 33, 41, 42, 46, 48, 49, 56, 59, 65, 68, 69, 73, 74, 77
Derby Borough Council Education Committee 89
Derby Hockey Club 43
Derby Royal Infirmary and Nightingale Nursing Home 89
Derby Sunday School League 43
Derbyshire County Council 74
Derbyshire Cricket Club 75
Diocesan Conference 65
Distinguished Flying Cross 82
District Commissioner of Scouts 60, 65
Doctor of Science 70
Ducks (nickname for type of train) 85

E

Egypt 75
Ellison, George 74
Engineering Diploma 9, 10
English Selection Board (hockey) 16

Euston 57, 58
Evesham
    Abbey Gates 54
    Almonry 1, 13
    Greenhill 8, 52
    High Street 7, 51, 74, 86
    Lanesfield 8, 52
    Mill Street 52
    Northwick Terrace 52
    Port Street 4, 5, 6, 85, 90
    Railway Hotel 86
    River Avon 6
    Swan Lane 51
    Victoria Avenue 50
    Workman Bridge 6, 53
Evesham Abbey 7
Evesham Cemetery 54
Evesham Hockey Club 15
Evesham Journal *35, 54*
Evesham Schools
    British School (Swan Lane) 51
    Deacle's School 51
    Miss Hill's (private school) 7
    National Schools 51
    Prince Henry's Grammar School 1, 7, 8, 23, 54, 82
Evesham Station 27, 60, 61, 63, 85

F

Farnborough 33, 34, 36, 37, 57
Flight Magazine *34, 36*
Follard, H.P. 34
Fowler Avenue 46
Fowler's Furniture Shop 7
France 25, 32, 46, 68

Freemantle 78
French, P.A. 36
Funeral... 80, 81

G

Gas Manager... 11, 12
Germany..32, 74, 79
Glasgow...68
Granet, Sir Guy..57

H

Haines, 'Woowey' 52
Hartley, Sir Harold.. 73, 74
Haslehurst, Samuel Rennie 50
Henrician (magazine) 7, 50, 51, 55, 64
Henrician Union 89
Horwich 10, 11, 13, 48, 56, 75
Hotel Cecil.. 35, 38
Hughes, George... 11, 47, 48, 55, 56, 59, 61
Hughes, Mary 5

I

Industrial Revolution... 1, 4, 9, 10, 82
Inspector of Materials 11
Institute of Metals.. 74, 89
Institute of Transport..89
Institution of Automobile Engineers.......................... 12, 42, 46, 89, 90
Institution of Civil Engineers... 12, 63
Institution of Locomotive Engineers 23, 25, 63, 89, 90
Institution of Locomotive Inspectors and Firemen 89
Institution of Mechanical Engineers..50
Institution of Mechanical Engineers 12, 37, 43, 46, 51, 63, 64, 65, 89, 90

International Railway Congress 46, 75, 89
International Railway Congress Association 74
International Railway Journal 23, 56

J

Johnson, Samuel 12

K

King George V 34, 35
Knighthood 35

L

Lickey Banker 31
Lickey incline 22, 41, 42, 83
Lieutenant-Colonel (honorary) 35
Life Membership of the Institution of Mechanical Engineers 74
Llangollen Railway Society 70
Lloyd George (Prime Minister) 32
Locomotive Superintendents 11
London 89

M

Madrid 89
Marriage 11
Marseilles 78
Mason Science College (Birmingham) 9, 23, 53
Maunsell, Richard 11, 46, 57
Mayflower 3
Mechanical Engineers 11, 23
Mendip Hills 29
Midland Counties League (cricket) 16
Miller Prize 89
Millwrights 11

Ministry of Munitions 32, 33, 37
Ministry of Transport 75, 79

N

National Certificates 64
New Zealand 78
Newcomb 10
North British Locomotive Company (NBL) 58
Nottingham Road Cemetery (Derby) 81

O

Oundle Public School 19

P

Palestine 75
Paris 74
Patriot (class) 69, 70, 75, 76
Pershore 4
Pittway, Edgar 52, 53
Pittway, Harold 52, 53
Pole, Sir Felix 57
Port Said 78

Q

Quakers 3, 4, 6, 7
Queen's Jubilee (1887) 8

R

Railway Accountants 11
Railway Act 47
Railway Engineering Gold Medal 89
Railway Mechanics Institute 10

Railway Rivalry 58
Railways
    Caledonian 47
    Great Western Railway (GWR) 3, 22, 26, 47, 57, 86
    Highland and Glasgow 47
    Lancashire and Yorkshire Railway 10, 11
    London and North Eastern Railway (LNER) 47, 57
    London and North Western (LNWR) 47, 68, 69
    London, Midland & Scottish (LMS) 14, 21, 47, 48, 49, 50,
        56, 57, 58, 59, 61, 63, 67, 68, 69, 83, 85, 86
    Midland Railway 2, 12, 14, 17, 19, 20, 22, 23, 27, 29, 41, 43,
        47, 67, 85
    North British Railway Company 72
    North British Railway Company (NBRC) 58
    Somerset and Dorset Joint Railway (S&DJR) 29, 30
    South Eastern and Chatham Railway 46
    South Western 47
    Southern Railway (SR) 46, 47, 57, 74
    Stockton and Darlington Railway 63
Reminiscences of an Old Boy 8
Rev. Basil Phillips 36
Rev. C. Herve 80
Rev. F.W. Holland 7, 8, 51, 52
Rev. H.C. Brocklehurst 80, 82
Rev. H.D. Hilliard 54
Rev. J.E. Dallimore 80
Rev. Robbins 54
Rev. Sealey Poole 8, 52
Rose Hill Street, Derby 13
Routes
    Ashchurch to Redditch 61
    Birmingham New Street to Ashchurch 83
    Birmingham to Ashchurch 60
    Bristol to Birmingham 41

    Bromsgrove to Blackwell 41
    Gloucester to Birmingham 83
    Oxford to Worcester 3
    Redditch to Evesham 83
    South Wales to the Midlands 60
    Toton to Brent 27, 60
Royal Aircraft Factory 2, 33, 34, 36
Royal Engineers 25
Royal Flying Corps 33
Royal Scot Class 58, 59, 67, 68, 69, 70, 71, 72, 75, 76

S

SE5a 34, 37
Shap Fell 57
Silk works in Evesham 4
Sir Henry Fowler Memorial Prize for Mathematics 50
Smith, Philip 11
Spondon 13, 19, 20, 25, 32, 35, 37, 38, 40, 54, 60, 65, 67, 77, 79, 80, 116
Spondon Cricket Club 19
Spondon Hall 43, 46, 65, 79, 80
Spondon Historical Society 43, 79
St Werburgh's Church (Spondon) 43, 46
St. Rollox 56
Stainer 29, 68, 74, 75
Stamp, Sir Josiah 73, 77
Steam Engineers 11
Stephenson 10, 63, 64
Sturch, Harry 52, 53
Swindon 57
Sydney 78

T

Telford Premium 89

The Homestead (Spondon) 19, 38, 43
The Times *58, 80*
Thompson, William (Bill) 19
Tractive Effort 26
Trevithick 10

U

University of Birmingham 9
University of Birmingham Engineering Society 23, 25, 89
University of Manchester 70, 89
Upton on Severn 4

V

Vickers 34
Victoria University 53

W

Watt Medal 12, 89
Webb Prize 89
Wheatcroft, Edward 52
Wheatcroft, George 52
Wheel Arrangement 27
Whitworth Exhibition 10
Wolseley 34
Worcester Chronicle *53*
Workman Exhibitioner 53
Workman Scholarship 53, 54
Wright, George 38, 40, 80

Z

Zurich 74